PROJECT REINVENTION

THE SOCIAL TIMELINE OF A MILLENNIAL

MAHFUZ CHOWDHURY

Copyright © 2017 Mahfuz Chowdhury
All rights reserved.
ISBN: 978-1-7750779-0-9

Website & Advertising by Candybox Marketing
Character Illustrations by Bitmoji
Publishing Assistance by Cheeky Kea Printworks

All rights reserved. No part of this book may be reproduced or transmitted in any form or by any means, electronic or mechanical, including photocopying, recording, or any information storage and retrieval system without prior written permission of the author.

For More From This Author:
https://projectreinvention.ca/
https://www.instagram.com/mahfuzc/
https://twitter.com/cmahfuz

Dedicated to every single individual that was a part of my personal development timeline.

The following is a timeline of a millennial.

This is my story.

TABLE OF CONTENTS

INTRODUCTION 1
CHAPTER 1: AN ABSOLUTE DISASTER 3
CHAPTER 2: THE PORTUGUESE 9
CHAPTER 3: GETTING SCHOOLED 15
CHAPTER 4: STARS ALIGN 19
CHAPTER 5: PROJECT REINVENTION 25
CHAPTER 6: STEP BY STEP 31
CHAPTER 7: WALKING THE PLANK 39
CHAPTER 8: DIVIDE AND CONQUER 45
CHAPTER 9: SWEET LIKE CANDY 53
CHAPTER 10: HERE IS MY BUSINESS CARD 59
CHAPTER 11: FACE-OFF 65
CHAPTER 12: SHOW TIME 71
CHAPTER 13: DRIVEN 77
CHAPTER 14: SHOEBOX 83
CHAPTER 15: GLORIOUS GENTLEMEN 89
CHAPTER 16: BEST MAN 93
CHAPTER 17: MONDAY MORNINGS 101
CHAPTER 18: CHATTERBOX STRIKES BACK 109
CHAPTER 19: HEARTBREAK 115
CHAPTER 20: LIKE A CHAMPION 121
CHAPTER 21: THREE-PEAT 127
ENDING REMARKS 135

INTRODUCTION

"Reinvent yourself."

This is usually the title of the presentation I would deliver at the beginning of my speaking events. The audience curiously looked up at my first slide and would soon learn how I revived my life after being shattered into a million pieces.

I would introduce myself as a national award winning marketer at Candybox Marketing, and flip through slides as I spoke about the different publications that wrote about my success.

"I don't say this to impress you." I continued. "What I hope to impress upon you is this..."

My next slide would showcase a resume that I created during my first year of college. The audience members were usually surprised to find that the only experience I had was serving coffee at Tim Horton's.

I would share the challenges that I faced over the years, including: immigrating to Canada with little money, collecting $30,000 in debt before being suspended from the university, pursuing a career with virtually no experience, recovering from heartbreak, and constantly failing after being put down my mental chatterbox.

Like my presentations, this book shares how an average millennial reinvented his life to become debt free, do what he loves every day, and find true happiness.

This is my social timeline.

CHAPTER 1

AN ABSOLUTE DISASTER

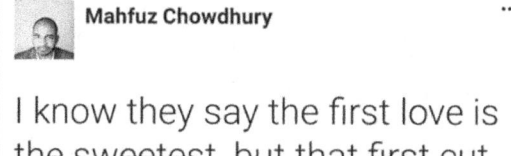

"This is an absolute disaster!"

My dad wasn't wrong.

He said it once more while rereading the bad news from the University of Toronto.

"Academic probation?! You are throwing your whole life away!"

I just kept looking down at my shaky feet. I couldn't bear looking into his disappointed eyes. It also doesn't help that my mom was right beside him trying to stop the waterfall pouring out of her eyes. I can't blame them for being this upset. I've officially hit rock bottom at the age of 22.

Getting suspended for poor grades was only the icing on this catastrophe-cake.

I would avoid opening bank statements that constantly reminded me about the $30,000 debt I acquired through student loans. It was hard to accept that 'academic probation' was the result of me attending classes while balancing two jobs and living on a shoe-string budget.

My typical day would start with serving coffee at a local Tim Horton's from 7am to 12pm, taking the city bus to attend classes between 1pm and 4pm, and then jumping back on the bus to a Montana's restaurant where I would prep enough ribs to last a lifetime. What did I have to show for this grind? $30,000 in debt and a vigorous caffeine addiction (I am actually okay with the latter. Hey, don't judge me!).

No need to sugar-coat this: I was a failure.

Once my dad finished giving his tough love, I stormed up to my room and was absolutely devastated.

On my way up, I pulled out my phone and noticed a missed call from my girlfriend. I knew she would be the best person to talk to. She would truly understand. I called her and explained the situation on the phone:

> To be honest, I don't even mind leaving the University

What do you mean?

> I was miserable there. I don't even know what I was doing taking business courses. I have no business being in business.

Lol. So, what did you want to do?

FOR YOUR READING PLEASURE:
Conversations in person, by phone, and through text messages will be displayed as chat boxes in this book.

> I don't know. I just know that I'm not happy with anything. I hated being the shy and quiet kid in every class, and I hated being tested on memorizing textbooks. No wonder I failed.

> So you are okay with being suspended?

> Part of me is okay with it. But my parents found out, and you know..

> I understand, babe.

Throughout our 3 year relationship, she had learned my entire life story. She knew about all the sacrifices my parents made by moving to Canada and giving up their comfortable life. While living in Saudi Arabia, my parents had a great life. My dad held a great position as a contract manager and my mom never had to work a day in her life. Moving to Canada to give my three brothers and me a better education, my dad ended up working in a labour intensive position at Home Depot and my mom worked as a housekeeper for several hotels. They gave up a great life for us.

This is why I wanted to do great things. That was my ultimate motivation.

> Don't worry, babe. You will figure it out. You always do.

> You know that's why I love you, right? 😊

I really hope she did.

Along with my parents, she made me want to try harder every day. We would spend date nights sketching out our dream house and planning our perfect future. I didn't have a plan but I had her, and that made me feel like I could do anything.

We would always laugh about the first time we met at Tim Horton's. She got hired part-time and I was in charge of training her. I was immediately swept away by this dorky brunette with the most beautiful smile and bubbly personality. She had this positive energy that always made me look forward to going to work. I just had to find out if she was available.

> Why is a cute girl like you single? What's wrong with you? 😊

> Lol. I don't know. Maybe I'm crazy and scare the boys away.

Bingo.

Since our first date, we made it our mission to go on wild adventures, including: getting lost in downtown Toronto or getting last minute tickets to random concerts.

I didn't make a lot of money, but I would always try to give her my best, whether I was showering her with gifts or getting her floor seats to a Taylor Swift concert (I have to admit, it was a pretty awesome show. I particularly respected how much attention she gave to every individual fan that lined up to meet her).

When our second anniversary came around, I knew that a typical date was not an option. While looking through different options, I ended up signing us up for a skydiving excursion. We even booked a videographer for the day.

"It's our two year anniversary," I said to the camera. "Instead of doing something crazy like a dinner and a movie, we decided to do something boring like jumping out of a plane at 14,000 feet."

We always talked about our future together so I bought her a promise ring to prove my commitment.

Simply put: she deserved the best.

What I wasn't prepared for was the six months that followed my academic probation. I thought the year away from school would give me more time to focus on her, but since the letter from the University, our entire relationship started sliding in a downward spiral. We argued regularly over the most irrelevant subjects, and before we knew it, disagreements turned into yelling, and yelling turned into swearing at each other.

After a few more miserable months, I decided that it would be best to end the relationship and go our separate ways.

We met up at her workplace and I found myself doing one of the hardest things I've ever had to do. She handed me her ring as we said our goodbyes.

"I really do wish the best for you," I said as I kissed her on the cheek for the last time. "Goodbye."

She wrapped her arms around my neck and cried louder than I've ever heard her cry. This became an extremely messy breakup. I stood there silently, flashbacking through all our amazing memories.

I was truly heartbroken.

Everything was going wrong and I was at my lowest point. I immediately reached out to the one person I trusted more than anyone.

I didn't know it at that time but this conversation was going to completely change my life.

CHAPTER 2

THE PORTUGUESE

"You did the right thing."

This was something I really needed to hear. I can always count on Mike to bring me up when I'm down.

I always thought that meeting my ex (something I never thought I'd call her) would be the greatest thing to come out of Tim Horton's but it was actually my friendship with Mike.

Whether he is Portuguese or not, I always saw Mike as my own brother.

People would often tell us that we were an odd duo.

Mike was a clean-shaved fit guy with light skin and I was a darker chubby guy with a chin-strap beard and little hair on my head. No matter how different we looked, our bond was unbreakable.

We started working at Tim Horton's at the same time and have been best friends since. It started with us finding out that we both loved the same superheroes and TV shows, and eventually started working out at the gym together, learning to break dance, and going on double-dates.

As shy and quiet as I was, he helped me break out of my shell. We would go out to parties and events so often that I naturally started to become more comfortable in public settings. Even though I didn't drink alcohol, he would make me feel comfortable in any venue. We always had friends coming in and out of our lives, but one thing that was consistent was our friendship.

Mike would put it best: "true boys are hard to come by."

Most importantly, we always looked out for each other. Whether it involved family, significant others, or day-to-day decisions, we would discuss it and create a plan. This is why I knew he was the guy to reach out to after the hell I just went through that year.

> I've know you long enough to know that you are smart enough to do anything you want.

> It's getting too hard to stay positive when everything is going downhill.

> I know its not easy, but it is possible. I promise you it is.

> I don't know what to do anymore. Where do I even start?

> You already know the answer. Do what we always do. Work out. Focus on yourself. Make yourself so awesome that she will look back and regret ruining your relationship. Work on yourself.

"Work on yourself". That is a message that will forever stick with me.

It was that moment that I realized that I could either curl up in my bed and mope for the rest of my life or get back on my feet to make a change.

I started going to the gym regularly to get in shape and start becoming happier with the way I look. My local Chapters became my go-to destination every weekend where I would spend hours reading personal development books to work on my mindset and outlook on life. I would also attend seminars and events that spoke about self-growth and confidence.

I found it surprising how difficult it was finding good materials that catered for students. Although there were a lot of great ideas, it was usually focused on helping aspiring entrepreneurs or people who were more financially (or emotionally) stable.

I found myself spending a lot of time and money searching for content that was relevant to me. This was frustrating, but I knew it would be worth it.

Sitting in my room, I spent days creating a collection of the best ideas and putting together an action plan. Learning the ideas was one thing, but executing them would make all the difference.

As Mike suggested, I was working on myself.

After spending an entire season working on myself, I felt like I was ready to take the next step. I decided to step away from the university path and look into colleges that focused on hands-on learning.

I had already learned the hard way that textbook memorization wasn't my forte so I decided to take another route.

While researching different colleges, I came across Sheridan College. The college had a great reputation for hands-on learning and also offered prestigious co-op programs that allowed students to gain experience while completing school.

> My parents aren't crazy about the idea of going to college instead of a university but I just know that it's the best decision for me.
>
> I completely agree. What program are you doing this time?
>
> I think I'm going to give business another shot. My university life should help me do a bit better in this program.
>
> I know that you will kill it in business. You are a natural.

Thanks for the vote of confidence, Mike.

After I applied and started walking away from Sheridan's registration desk, I realized that my mentality was very different this time around. When I applied to the University of Toronto (UofT), I simply wanted to graduate as quickly as possible so that I could stop going to school. This time I felt eager to learn and really get the most out of the experience.

The night before school, I sat in my room and started preparing all my school supplies (like all cool last-minute kids do). Suddenly, a realization struck me like lightning. I realized that no one would know who I was. No one knew a thing about my past and my downfalls. I could literally walk in and be anyone I wanted to be.

This realization opened my eyes to many opportunities. I spent the entire summer working on myself and becoming the best me. It was time to put this to the test.

I made an action plan to start the first year on the right foot. No more 'Shy Mahfuz'. It was time to get more involved and break out of my shell. I knew that the best way to grow was by getting out of my comfort zone.

After being down the entire year, it was refreshing getting this excited about something again. To me: it wasn't just about going back to school. It was about a fresh start.

I was happy with my action plan and went to bed with a smile on my face.

It was time to go back to school.

CHAPTER 3

GETTING SCHOOLED

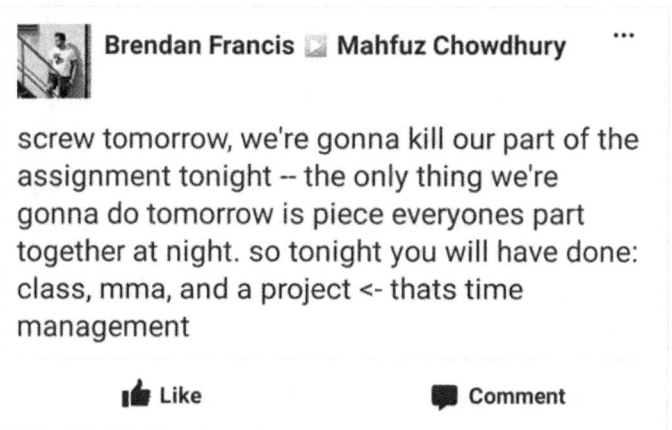

Admittedly, the first day of college felt strange. It was weird being back in a school environment. I kept hoping that the eagerness for a fresh start would overpower the nerves. It helped that there were many other students that filled the hallways with excitement.

I was still concerned about my program choice since I still wasn't sure if I wanted to pursue the business path.

"What does business even mean?" I thought to myself. "There are so many different sections in business. Do I just want to be an entrepreneur?" I decided that I would figure it out as I went.

My first class was 'Marketing 101'. As I started walking into the classroom, I reminded myself to put the 'New Mahfuz' forward.

I took a seat beside someone who was plugging in his laptop.

> This is a serious change from university. I sat in a lecture hall of 500 students at UofT, this is what, like 30 students?

> Lol. Yo I went to UofT too! Brendan nice to meet you.

Brendan initially seemed quiet and reserved, but I couldn't be more wrong. He was very smart and down to earth. Brendan shared his passion for sales and marketing, which was easy to believe after meeting his confident personality. We hit it off right away and I immediately felt comfortable being in class.

Few minutes later, our professor walked into the room to kick off the morning.

"Keith is the name", he introduced himself. "Welcome to Sheridan College."

Keith came in with a lot of energy and really engaged the classroom. What really captivated me was his burning passion for marketing. He spent most of the morning sharing stories and his personal experience with marketing. I was curious to learn more.

Throughout the week, we took all the other required courses for the Business program but my mind kept drifting back to marketing. I was excited to learn more each week.

Over the next few weeks, Keith put us into groups for different activities. He asked us to put together a marketing strategy for fictional products and present it to the class.

It was at that moment I fell in love with Marketing.

I enjoyed engaging the creative part of my brain to come up with fun and practical ideas. It excited me thinking about bringing these ideas to life for a real business.

When it came to presenting the ideas, the group nominated me to be the speaker. As nervous as I was, I quickly triggered the 'New Mahfuz' mentality, stood up and delivered a short presentation.

I spoke about creating a marketing model where employees would be rewarded for building a team and generating sales.

After I finished sharing our ideas, I looked around the room as everyone stared in silence (picture the 'deer in headlights' look).

"Way to go, Mahfuz. You totally crashed and burned!" I silently screamed in my head.

"We have to go after that?!" said the next group that was preparing to present.

"You got the silver tongue, man!" Brendan said enthusiastically as I took my seat.

Turns out, I delivered a presentation so good that it stunned the class.

As the next group started speaking, I leaned back on my seat and wondered if I just discovered an untapped talent.

Until then, the last time I did any public speaking was in my Grade 8 English class where I wore a bunch of garbage bags to dress up as a bat for my book report presentation (don't ask!). Public speaking was foreign to me, but all I knew was that it was a thrilling feeling.

As weeks went by, I kept discussing that feeling with Brendan.

> The biggest fear in the world in public speaking, you know. You're already ahead of the game.

> I am starting to feel like Marketing and public speaking might be my calling.

> If anyone can do it, it would be you.

This first year of college was a major eye opener for me. It made me realize what career path was right for me. I immediately opted into the Marketing program and exhaled a sigh of relief, as for the first time in my life, I finally knew what I wanted to pursue.

Our first co-op term was right around the corner and it was time to find somewhere to work for the next three months.

I looked at the job board and came across Sheridan College's 'Student Recruitment Associate' position.

I started to read the job description and was intrigued by the idea of giving campus tours and promoting what Sheridan had to offer. It seemed like a good mix of public speaking and marketing. I decided to give it a shot and apply.

I was offered the position shortly after the interview process and got an immediate feeling of overwhelming joy. For that split moment, I didn't think about my ex.

"A fresh start," I kept reminding myself.

Little did I know, taking this position was one of the best decisions I'd ever make.

CHAPTER 4

STARS ALIGN

"You must be Mahfuz," Angela welcomed me with a big smile. "I am so excited to work with you!"

Angela was the student recruitment manager at the campus. I would be working with her throughout the work term. Angela's bubbly personality made it easy for me to be myself at work.

Every week, students and parents would visit the college campus to learn about what we had to offer.

I always looked forward to providing a tour to improve my public speaking skills. Although I was given a script, I would add my personality to make it my own. I started mixing in my personal stories and experience within the script, to really put the campus visitors at ease.

The visitors were given the opportunity to provide written feedback at the end of every tour. Although I was very flattered by all the positive feedback, what really stood out to me was how much my personal stories resonated with them.

I kept skimming through the feedback:

"Mahfuz's stories made me realize that this was the right college for me!"

"I was debating between going to college or university but Mahfuz's experience sold me on Sheridan!"

I started to learn about the power of personal storytelling. I learned that people remember stories more than they remember facts. I made note to include more personal stories in all my future speaking events.

Over the next week, Angela introduced me to another side of my job. She mentioned that I will also be managing a team of forty Sheridan students who will be providing tours for their specific programs. We called this group the Sheridan STARs (student admission representatives).

Each day, members of STARs would visit my office and introduce themselves. I started to bond with them and learned about their different career goals.

They all had different stories, different dreams, and continuously inspired me every single day. I knew that we would all be friends by the end of my work term.

It was a slow afternoon so I spent some extra time in my office, scheduling in campus tours. I heard a knock on the door and in walks in a blond guy, wearing all black clothes and a business jacket.

"Hi, I'm Mark. I just got hired as a STAR and they said you will be training me."

Mark was enrolled in the theatre program but I probably could have guessed that based on how energetic and animated he was.

> Would it be okay if I did the tour in a thick British accent? We would seem like the most elegant school ever!

> Only if you switch up your accent half-way to throw them off. I'm firing you if they don't come back confused by the end of the tour 😊

Fifteen minutes of laughs later, I came to the conclusion that Mark was the funniest guy I had ever met. After wiping away the tears from laughing, we decided to go to the weekly pub night with other STARs members and have been great friends since.

During the same week, another knock opened the door to an amazing friendship with Argyle.

Describing Argyle can be summarized by the way he answered one question during a group activity:

> What do you see when you look in the mirror?

> I see a small Filipino guy with a goal.

Nailed it.

Argyle is one of the most hardworking, ambitious, and humble person I know. Pursuing a career as a computer system analyst, he constantly found ways to innovate while helping others along the way. I haven't met a single person that hasn't gotten along with Argyle after meeting him.

That afternoon, there was one final knock (probably should have just removed the door by now). I see a taller guy walking in with a bright coloured t-shirt and a silicone wristband. He reached out to shake my hand.

"Hey, I'm Marc." (Yes, with a 'c')

I really connected with Marc because he had a very similar story to mine. He went through a series of challenges and was on his own personal development journey. He also happened to be studying Marketing.

"It's really impressive." I commended him. "We were both shattered into a million pieces and completely reinvented ourselves."

'Reinvention'. I was beginning to like that word.

We both agreed that most books, videos, and events were directed at business owners, and that it was very difficult to find good personal development content that are geared towards students. At that instant moment, a giant light bulb switched on above our heads.

> We should start our own personal development website for students.

> I am actually down. I have been wanting to do something like this for a while now.

> What should we call it?

After pondering about how much the both of us reinvented ourselves, I smiled.

"How about Project Reinvention?"

CHAPTER 5

PROJECT REINVENTION

'Project Reinvention's mission is to educate and inspire students to grow to their full potential.'

This was the first thing Marc and I wrote down during our brainstorming session. We looked around the library and couldn't wait to introduce this concept to everyone sitting around us.

I pulled out my collection of personal development ideas and told Marc about how much time and money I spent finding the best content for the notebook.

> Students will love this because they won't need to spend all that time or break the bank.

> They will also be able to relate to all the challenges we faced and learn about how we overcame them.

The best thing about giving birth to this concept was that we didn't talk about making money. Instead of focusing on monetizing through Project Reinvention, we were simply passionate about helping others grow. Everything we would do was all about helping others.

Since 'ProjectReinvention.com' was already taken, we decided to make our website address 'YourReinvention.com' to reiterate that the website was made for the visitors.

We spent the day jotting down all the different ways we could share our ideas with students. We decided that we would post two blog articles each week and start recording podcasts. We decided that we would also connect with students directly through Facebook, Twitter, and by speaking at events.

'Speaking at events'; this was what I was the most excited about.

Reading blogs would be insightful, but I knew that nothing would help more than personally reaching out to students and engaging them in a conversation.

Over the next few weeks, Marc and I spent hours crafting our new website. We researched other personal development websites and tried to replicate them.

"We should do things differently", I suggested. "We want to stand out in a crowd."

Most of the websites we found would lead in by discussing who they were, what they offered, and then provide links to help the students get started.

"Why waste the first page by just bragging about yourself" I thought. We decided to move the spotlight away from us and instead start providing good content right away.

'Personal Development for Students'. We added this slogan to the top of the site. This is the only thing they need to know about us. The rest of the homepage shared our most recent blog articles and links to our podcast. If students are coming to our website for great ideas, we should make it as easy as possible for them to find it.

We reached out to Argyle to help create the logo for Project Reinvention.

> We want the logo to spark a part of the reader's brain that makes them change their life for the better.

> How about a light bulb?

Boom!

A few days later, Argyle stepped into my office with a draft of the logo.

"Simple but significant," I said. "Love it!"

Once we were happy with the look of our website, Marc and I uploaded four blog articles and one podcast. This way, the students would have some good content when they visited on the first day.

We sat back, looked at each other, and smiled. The website was ready.

We pushed the 'launch website' button together and it became a moment I would never forget.

Marc and I gathered our group of friends and went to a local bar. We shared the good news, followed by high fives all around. It was encouraging to see everyone just as excited as we were.

"This is going to be huge!" Mark said out loud.

"I will tell everyone I know!" Argyle announced.

I sat at the table, gazing out the window of possibilities. Marc and I didn't have a lot of online marketing experience, but we had a burning desire to do what it took to make it work.

The next morning, I went back to my office to prepare for the upcoming campus tour. As parents and students gathered around, I started to feel a sharp burn in my eyes and immediately ran to the bathroom.

I figured that my contact lens may be out of place so I rinsed my eyes and readjusted the lens.

I kicked off the tour with blood-shot red eyes and kept hoping it would clear up by the end of the day. Half way through the tour, my vision became irritated and I noticed that my eyes were automatically closing shut. As hard as I tried to open them, it would fight back. I wouldn't wish this excruciating pain on my worst enemy.

After apologizing to my tour group, I asked another colleague to take over and ran back to the bathroom. Saying that 'I was freaking out' would be an understatement.

I rapidly flushed water into my eyes and then stumbled my way into the college's health clinic. They were kind enough to offer me eye drops and let me lay down for an hour. I laid there in darkness wondering: Why is this happening? Why me?

My dad came down to the campus and drove me to the nearest walk-in clinic. I can always count on dad.

The doctor stated that I was suffering from an eye infection and that I would be fine after a few days. As someone who thought he was going blind, this was extremely pleasant to hear.

Ironically, the next few days was an eye opener (see what I did there?). I laid in bed and felt helpless. It gave me a lot of time to reflect on how much things have changed over the last year. I thought about how hard I was on myself during the most difficult time of my life.

"I was such a loser." I chuckled to myself.

I then started to think about all the amazing people around me and how lucky I was to have them. My circle of friends was not large but I wouldn't have it any other way. This all started because of my conversation with Mike.

"Thanks Mike." I muttered without realizing how weird it was talking to myself.

I also realized how lucky I was to have the most incredible parents. Even as I laid there, they would regularly check on me or bring up my favourite meals. They were tough on me, but I knew it was because they wanted me to succeed. Even when they disagreed, they would support my decision every step of the way.

I was truly blessed.

As my eyes started to heal, I decided to use my time efficiently and create content for the website.

"The day I went blind," I said out loud as I typed out the title to my newest blog.

I spent the rest of the night sharing my enlightening experience from the past few days. I wrote about 'gratitude' and how important it was to take some time to look back and appreciate your growth.

I published it on our live website and then closed the laptop.

I was soon going to learn that this article single-handedly skyrocketed the success of Project Reinvention.

CHAPTER 6

STEP BY STEP

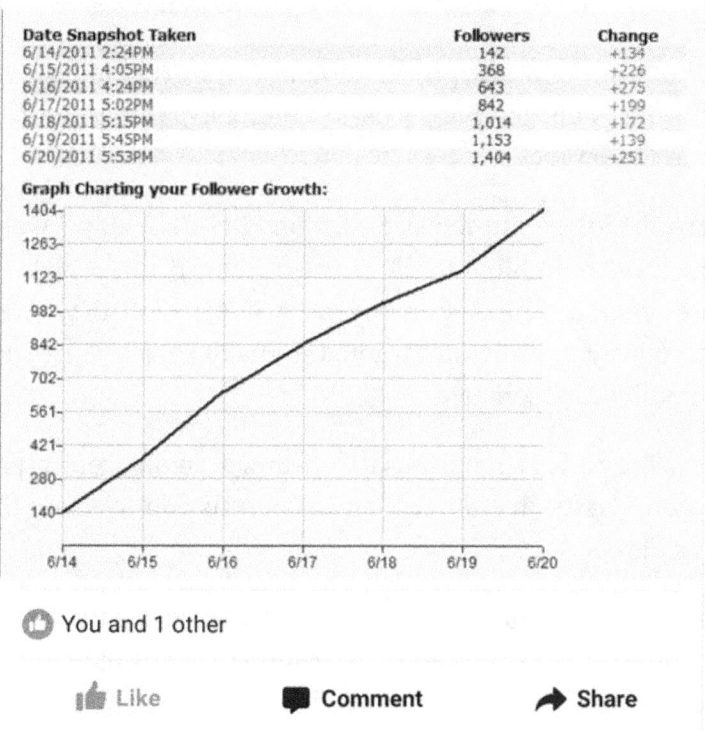

"Bro, Project Reinvention is exploding!" Marc called me up one afternoon.

I realized that we had been so involved in producing good content for the website that we completely forgot to review the stats.

Nothing prepared us for the shocking stats we found in the back-end of our website.

> 1000 subscribers in the first five days!

> Our website was receiving hundreds of hits each day, with people visiting from over 20 countries.

> Hey Marc, guess what? We are universal!

It was humbling to see people around the world finding value on our website. This motivated us to continue putting our heart and soul into the project.

As I dived further into the stats, I found that 'The day I went blind' was the most read blog article. I wasn't sure if this was happening because people found tremendous value or if they were just freaked out by the title and wanted to make sure I was okay. I just knew that I was fascinated.

At the same time, I received a well-timed email from a professor from a university in Iran, asking for permission to share this blog with his class.

"Imagine that," I thought to myself. "A letter that I wrote, half-blind is now being showcased on the other side of the world."

 **Mahfuz Chowdhury**

Got this email from a professor in Iran that will be sharing one of my blogs with his University students. It is amazing to see how a blog from my bedroom can go half way across the world!

Dear **Mahfuz Chowdhury**

Thanks god because of your healthy eyes. I read your text about the day you went blind in internet. Your experience was so nice and wonderful. Thank you because of writing your experience. I learn many things from that.

I will have a lecture about "blindness". After reading your text of experience, I decided to tell it in my lecture.

I would be so glad to see your image and know your field of study and your country.

Thank You. Have a wisely, lovely and actively life...

 Dennis Yu and 16 others   4 Comments

👍 Like   💬 Comment   ➤ Share

The reinvention rush didn't end there, over the next four days we acquired another thousand subscribers. I don't think a single minute flew by without me thinking about how amazing this project was becoming.

A few days later, I received a message from Brad, someone from Vancouver who came across my website, who was about to make a drastic change in his life.

"I did love the job. I did. Just that it was repetitive, took no thought" Brad wrote. "So that morning, I called work and told them I have lost the drive. As the old saying goes, money does not buy happiness".

He went on explaining how he wanted to leave his position and wanted to pursue a career as a professional draftsman. He said that our website was what motivated him to make a change.

This put me in a very tough position as I wasn't prepared to encourage someone into leaving a high-paying job. It worried me to think that his life was in my hands. My response needed to be carefully crafted. Instead of making the big decision for him, I spoke to him about weighing out the pros and cons to determine the best decision for him.

Brad made the decision to resign and I spent a lot of time preparing him for interviews to ensure that he truly got what he wanted.

I would follow up with him later to find out that he landed the position as a draftsman for an amazing engineering company. The company even offered to send Brad to get his architectural autoCAD.

"Thank you for your personal message to me and a website full of helpful direction, and here's to the future," Brad wrote. "I can only hope more people read what you have put out and are able to move forward using that info."

At that very moment, I knew with every fibre in my body that our ideas were good for everyone.

No more doubts; I truly believed in reinvention.

My work term was wrapping up and I looked forward to going back to class and focus on growing Project Reinvention.

Crowds of high school students swarmed into the campus to kick off their STEPs event. STEPs stood for: Student Transition Exchange Program. This would involve the students spending the week at the college's residence and participating in daily activities.

For one of the activities, students were given the opportunity to take a tour of the campus. Angela asked me to stay behind after-hours to give the students a personal tour.

"They are going to learn so much from your experience," she said with joy.

At 5pm, I walked into the residence building and was surprised to be greeted by Kavita, an old classmate that I haven't seen since high school.

> Kavita? Oh my god! What are you doing here?

> Mahfuz! I am helping facilitate the week with all the high school students.

> Well, I hope you are ready for the best tour of your life 😊

> Nice job, buddy. Now my expectations are through the roof!

I showed the students around the campus and was impressed by how attentive they all were.

They would laugh at my corny jokes and asked great questions. I really enjoyed this group.

At the end of the tour, Kavita asked me to join the group for dinner so that we could catch up.

I sat in a large dinner room and was enthusiastically greeted by all the high school students. I really appreciated how welcoming this group was.

Suddenly, another light bulb appeared over my head.

> **Hey Kavita, do you have any openings for a speaking event this week?**
>
> What do you mean?
>
> **A friend and I started a program to help students with personal growth. Would love to do a seminar to talk to them.**
>
> So, what would you talk about?
>
> **..I don't know.**

I really didn't. I hadn't done this before but knew that Marc and I had enough ideas to put something together.

She said that the STEPs group had a very busy week but would talk to her supervisors about it. I didn't expect much but I appreciated the gesture. I gave Marc the heads up and he said he was waiting in anticipation.

The next morning, I received a phone call from Kavita:

> Hey, are you free tonight?
>
> **Are you asking me out, Kavita? You should know that I'm very high maintenance.**
>
> Lol! I spoke to my supervisor and she said that you could speak to the students.
>
> **Amazing! When?**
>
> Can you do tonight?
>
> **It's a date!**

I hung up and fumbled the phone in excitement as I dialed Marc's phone number.

"Suit up, sir." I barely got the next words out. "Tonight is the night."

CHAPTER 7

WALKING THE PLANK

"What are you doing tonight?"

We started calling up friends to attend our first ever Project Reinvention seminar. To get past our nerves, we figured it would help seeing familiar faces in the crowd.

Brendan, Mark, and Argyle confirmed that they would be attending to cheer us on.

After work, I went home to change. I shuffled through my closet and came to realize that I didn't own a lot of formal clothes. A black dress shirt and dress pants were really my only options, so I threw on a bright red tie to avoid looking like I was attending a funeral.

"Maybe I am dressing up for Project Reinvention's funeral."

My negative chatterbox started to take control. I started worrying about freaking out and freezing up on stage.

"What if it doesn't go well? What if everyone finds out we failed and we never get invited to speak again?"

My mental chatterbox was quickly becoming my worst enemy.

I took a minute to meditate and think about everything I have learned through my personal growth. I thought about how much our advice helped Brad change his life, and many others like him.

"This seminar will change their lives!" I said out loud and immediately walked out of my house.

Marc and I met up with friends in front of the campus residence.

"This is awesome." I said as I greeted them. "We are like a rock band that brings their own fans to their shows."

Kavita greeted us at the entrance and I introduced her to my friends.

> The students are so excited to see you again!
>
> Kavita, I just wanted to thank you for taking a chance on us. I hope you know this is our first ever seminar.
>
> Your first? I didn't know that. Now I'm cancelling the event. ☺

We walked into the conference room and started setting up our presentation. Some teachers also attended the seminar out of curiosity.

Argyle volunteered to film the presentation so that we could share the footage with our website subscribers.

Marc and I quickly strategized and decided that we would speak one at a time. We both agreed that I should go first.

As Marc was testing the microphone, I was impressed by how comfortable he seemed. I looked around the room and watched as all students arranged their chairs, preparing for us to blow their minds. My heart started pumping with anxiety. I never understood how speakers did this so naturally. How was a shy guy like me going to speak in a room full of people?

"We've already come this far," I thought to myself. "We got this!"

As I was getting mentally prepared, I thought back to all the personal growth seminars I attended and remembered how the speakers would get introduced by the host. It would build their credibility and hype up the audience.

Naturally, the master entertainer came to mind. With his experience in theatre, this should be a walk in the park. I approached Mark and asked him to do a quick introduction to get the crowd excited. He appreciated the opportunity, but I knew that I would appreciate it much more.

Mark stood in front of the room and got everyone's attention. He made the audience laugh and spoke about how Project Reinvention has helped him in every aspect of his life. He then gloated about our friendship before asking the crowd to give a round of applause as I walked up to the front.

"Wow. With an introduction like that, I have to sound smart now, don't I?" I started.

The crowd laughed. This immediately silenced my chatterbox and put me at ease.

"I want you all to use your imagination and picture a plank of wood in the room, a very thin but long plank". I can see the crowd engaged as I created this visual.

"Now, picture this plank sitting between the roofs of two very tall buildings. How many of you would cross this plank if I gave you a $100?"

The students laughed as a few hands went up in the crowd.

"Really? Okay, now what if the other building was on fire. How many of you would still cross this plank?"

Only a couple hands went up.

"Okay, a few brave souls that really need the $100s"

The crowd laughed again. This was getting good.

"Now I want you to picture someone you love in the burning building. Someone who has always been there for you. Jokes aside, even if I took away the $100 from the table, how many of you would cross this plank to save their lives?"

Everyone in the room quickly threw their hands up in the air. The teachers smiled as they were content by the response.

"This is your WHY," I continued. "This is your burning desire. I want every one of you to know that if you want something bad enough, there are no challenges or obstacles that will stop you from getting it."

The students were starting to get more serious. I could see that they were really taking the message in.

"My WHY is my mother."

I shared my mom's struggle and talked about how she gave up a great life for me.

"This is why I knew that I would never quit. When times got hard, I kept moving forward because I could never look my mother in the eye and tell her that I was giving up on her. Discover your burning desire and become amazed by how motivated you are every single day."

After sharing my personal story and a few more ideas, I passed the torch by introducing Marc and calling him to the front of the room for his part of the presentation.

As I took my seat, I started to feel really good about how the seminar was going. I hadn't felt that thrilled since I stood up to present our solutions during Keith's Marketing class.

Marc also delivered a great presentation and the crowd roared in applause as we both stood in front of the room and thanked them for listening.

I shook Marc's hand and he had the same smug look on his face as I did. I knew we were both thinking the same thing: "We did it!"

As we were packing up, I turned around to find a line up of students who wanted to personally meet us. Marc and I were both flattered.

I took a page out of Taylor Swift's book and wanted to give each student a hundred percent of my attention. No matter how many people were waiting to meet us, I would take my time speaking to each individual. I wanted each student to feel like we were the only ones in the room.

The first one in line approached with tears in her eyes. She shook my hand and introduced herself.

"I wish I met you 3 years ago," she said while trying to hold back her tears. "Everything was going wrong in my life and I really needed to hear something like this."

I could relate.

She made me realize that there are many people who are going through challenges similar to what I had been through. This encounter would stay with me forever.

I consoled and encouraged her to use what she learned and take action.

"I promise you, it only takes one season to turn your life from tragic to magic".

As we finished meeting everyone in line, Kavita and the teachers showered us with compliments. They asked us to come back next week to speak to the high school students that are attending the STEPs program in the other campus. We graciously accepted.

The momentum had begun.

CHAPTER 8

DIVIDE AND CONQUER

"Our next presentation should always be our best presentation."

This was the mentality we had to strive for greatness.

I sat in my living room couch and uploaded Argyle's video to my laptop. It was time to become my own harshest critic.

While watching the video, I wrote down things to improve for future presentations. I noted that I needed to move around the room with purpose and pause frequently to let the messages resonate with the audience. I also eliminated material that didn't seem to fly well and emphasized the ones that the audience enjoyed.

I reached out to Mark for some theatre performance advice. Mark and I would frequently bounce ideas back and forth from our experience. Mark would use his theatre expertise to give me advice about public speaking and engaging the audience. I would provide marketing ideas to help Mark stand out in a crowd of actors and recommend different ways he can promote himself.

I started to become a better speaker each day by putting Mark's advice to practice. Whether it involved rehearsing in an empty room or recording in front of a camera, I focused on continual improvement.

"Public speaking is an art," I told Mark. "I want to work on my craft."

The second STEPs presentation was an incredible success. I decided to bring along an audio recorder so that I could continue improving based on my performance.

The future was looking bright for Marc and me.

...Or was it?

Marc and I had very similar goals but our approach was different. We found ourselves frequently arguing about our ideas.

"We should do our podcasts together instead of individually," Marc would suggest. "That way, they can learn from both of us."

"This isn't necessary," I quickly rejected his idea. "We have different stories and messages and should share them independently."

Things were going well and I wasn't prepared to ruin it by changing our methods.

After rejecting his third idea, Marc finally put his foot down.

> You're very head strong. Often more head strong then I am which is impressively hard to come across.

> Sorry man. This is all new to me. I am just trying to make my ideas work.

> I don't feel like a leader in this company regardless of how many times you tell me that I am a CEO and that I show initiative.

> I agree that I can be stubborn. Sometimes I need to be reminded when I am getting out of line.

> One of the things that really bothers me about you is that you never admit that you're wrong.

Marc wasn't wrong. I should've realized that the success of Project Reinvention was getting to my head. I made a lot of executive decisions without consulting him. Since I kept acting on my instincts, I just assumed that he would be on board with it.

After a few more arguments, Marc finally decided that he wanted to go separate ways.

"I want to do my own thing," he announced. "You can keep Project Reinvention. I will start from scratch."

My heart sunk.

We put our heart and soul into this. I never even entertained the idea of doing this initiative by myself. How could he be willing to throw it all away?

I knew there was nothing I could say to change his mind, and as furious as I was, I shook his hand and wished him the best of luck.

My dad's words echoed in my head: "this is an absolute disaster!"

I wasn't sure if Project Reinvention would work without Marc's help. He was instrumental to the success of the project.

"Well, it was fun while it lasted." I thought to myself.

Over the next few weeks, Project Reinvention was on hiatus. No new blogs, no posts on social media, we practically evaporated overnight. I started to lose motivation.

I even received an email from Jean, a teacher who attended the STEPs seminar, and was invited to speak to college students about personal growth. I wasn't prepared to respond back. I wasn't ready to do it without Marc.

"You should just do this on your own," Brendan said after hearing about my divorce with Marc. "You came this far and have a huge community. Just keep grinding."

He had a point, but I wasn't finished grieving.

I spent the night clearing my email inbox and came across all the amazing letters I received from visitors.

"I love your page and what you guys are doing. Wonderful and powerful stuff. You guys have actually sparked new life into me. I hope this project will help others like it helped me."

"What you do is very inspiring man. Truly good luck with everything and hope to keep in touch with you!"

"I just wanted to tell you that you inspire me to quite an extent. I find you truly as an aspiring role model."

I was humbled. I quickly felt my arrogance fading away.

These amazing letters made me think about how Project Reinvention helped Brad change career paths and do something he absolutely loved. We have created tremendous positive change around the world and it wouldn't have been possible without the work we put in.

I wasn't ready to quit.

The hesitation was over. I immediately responded back to Jean and accepted the invitation.

The momentum continued to grow. Every event I spoke at would result in another invitation. There was always someone in every audience that wanted me to share my story with their group.

I found myself speaking at dozens of events over the next two months. Different colleges and high schools learned about my initiative and wanted to learn more. The international office wanted me to speak to students about overcoming challenges. Entrepreneurship events would ask me to teach business owners how to make their websites perform as well as Project Reinvention. The education camp invited me to help teachers engage their students. Co-op programs wanted me to speak to aspiring students about applying what they learn during their work terms. Even Angela invited me to speak to her students at the next Sheridan STARs Orientation.

What I wasn't prepared for was the cheques that would arrive in my mailbox. Events started paying for my time.

"I am officially a professional speaker." I thought with a smile as I flipped through the mail.

Notifications kept flying in, as event attendees shared how much they gained from my talks. This was what motivated me to keep going every day. I took the time responding back to every single message to remind them how much their encouragement meant to me.

"How would you like to get featured on the news?" One of the messages read.

Emma was a journalism student and wanted to write an article about Project Reinvention.

I invited her to do the interview over a cup of coffee. I wanted to get comfortable with her so that I could deliver all the right messages for the article.

> In 1996, we moved from Saudi Arabia to Canada. My dad gave away an amazing job, and my mom had never worked a day in her life. When we came to Canada, she started doing housekeeping.

That must be tough.

> It really was. When I wasn't doing well, she started wondering why she sacrificed everything. That was my wake-up call.

What did you do?

> I decided that I was going to do everything I can to change myself for the better, to show my parents it was worth it.

The interview was going well. Emma continued asking great questions.

Why 'Project Reinvention'?

> The reinvention part referred to helping students change. I want it to be that one-stop-shop for all personal development needs.

And the 'project'?

> Students can relate to projects as they do them all their lives. Reinventing was just another project. Also, I am a big fan of Fight Club and always loved their idea of 'Project Mayhem'.

She quickly interrupted me by reminding me about the first rule of Fight Club.

The article came out a few days later, and I read the title: "Positive change just a click away".

CHAPTER 9

SWEET LIKE CANDY

"It's that time of the year again."

Jenny, the co-op coordinator, announced to the class as we were preparing to apply for our second work term.

As much as I loved working with Angela and the Sheridan STARs, I was eager to find a business that would benefit from my digital marketing experience. My Project Reinvention experience allowed me to learn about using social media tools and building successful websites. These are skills that businesses could really use.

A few years ago, I would have been nervous about applying for marketing firms with only coffee-serving experience. After putting in the work to build my experience, I felt like I was ready.

Jenny spoke about the advantages of using LinkedIn to connect with employers. I couldn't wait to get started.

After creating my business profile on LinkedIn, I started searching for digital marketing firms.

I came across a profile that immediately caught my eye.

"Darrell Keezer," I read out loud. "Meet your newest employee." I was wishful thinking.

I continued reading and learned that he was the owner of a firm called Candybox Marketing. He also went to Sheridan College and had similar interests.

Darrell's profile had my attention because it was evident how much he loved marketing. He started Candybox Marketing shortly after completing college and had a strong desire to help businesses.

It would be amazing working for someone as passionate as Darrell. If anything, I was hoping he would at least recommend a business worth applying for.

I added Darrell on LinkedIn, followed by a personal note:

"Thanks for accepting my LinkedIn invite!

I am currently completing my second year at Sheridan College Business Marketing Program. I can tell by your experience that you have a lot of expertise in this field, and was wondering if you could recommend a local company that would be a good choice for my upcoming Co-op Work Term.

Thanks a million, I really appreciate any help that you can offer."

I could barely continue researching other employers before a response from Darrell hit my inbox. He shared his cell phone number and asked me to call him.

"Meet me at our local Starbucks in 30 minutes. I might be able to help." He said after I introduced myself in the phone call.

I started hesitating.

The Starbucks he wanted to meet at was almost an hour away by foot. I didn't own a car and there was no bus in sight. Putting all my money towards my $30,000 debt, I didn't even have enough to hail a cab. I continued hesitating.

"Maybe I should cancel the meeting," my mental chatterbox tried to talk me out of it. "I can at least try to reschedule."

I was worried that this opportunity wouldn't be available for long, so I silenced my chatterbox.

I had a gut feeling that this was the right meeting for me. Darrell was generous enough to offer help and I wasn't about to screw this up.

Instead of making excuses, I immediately dove into my closet to find my favourite running shoes. I was determined to make this work.

The run wasn't pleasant. It was raining outside and I quickly realized how out of shape I was.

By some type of miracle, I managed to make it to our meeting with two minutes to spare. Wiping the sweat off my forehead, I convinced myself that the sweat might just make me seem desperate enough for Darrell to hire me.

I walked into Starbucks and saw a young well-dressed man sitting in the back of the store.

> Nice to meet you. Please have a seat.

> Thank you very much for taking the time out to help a fellow Sheridan student.

Darrell shared a bit about his entrepreneurship journey and I was immediately hooked.

"I was let go by an IT company and decided to take control of my own future by starting Candybox Marketing."

What really caught my attention was Darrell's storytelling style. He spoke in a way that made me understand his life goals and purpose. He also listened attentively every time I spoke. He was a genuinely good guy.

I started to share about my success with Project Reinvention but it seemed like he already did his homework.

> The stats are very impressive. How did you grow Project Reinvention?

> I didn't pay much attention to the stats. I just focused on grinding and helping students.

Darrell shared his vision for a new pilot project. He wanted Candybox to host monthly workshops to help businesses get started with social media marketing.

He wanted me to promote and conduct these workshops. I loved the idea of using my marketing and public speaking experience at the same time. This was an ideal position.

"I believe in working mobile," Darrell continued. "You can work from wherever you are most comfortable to eliminate distractions." I really respected this mentality.

Candybox Marketing was still a fairly new company. It consisted of 3 team members and everyone worked from different locations. I got excited to work with a start up and build it up from the ground floor.

> This sounds like an amazing opportunity. When can I start?

> How about next week?

"The newest member of Candybox Marketing"; Sounds pretty sweet.

CHAPTER 10

HERE IS MY BUSINESS CARD

"That's a really big deal. Congratulations!"

Jenny and my classmates cheered me on as I shared the story about landing a co-op position with Candybox Marketing.

"Keep going over and beyond to show your value for Darrell," Brendan advised. "Before you know, you will be working as a top executive at Candybox."

Over the next few days, other students started announcing the names of the companies they would be working with.

"I will be working at Scotiabank," Stephanie shared enthusiastically with her classmates.

"You are looking at the newest Marketing Assistant at a top HVAC company!" Ashley revealed while we worked together on a group project. We all couldn't wait to get started.

The next morning, Darrell showed up at my doorstep and dropped off five cases of business cards.

"You'll need this for all the networking events you will be attending."

It became official. I was so excited that I immediately took photos of the business cards and shared them on Facebook.

"Do what I told you and you'll be far ahead of the game homie!" Brendan immediately commented.

I replied back: "Always keeping that advice on the top of my mind. Thanks bro!"

That weekend, I was invited to share some marketing strategies on a live webinar.

The host came across my success with Project Reinvention and asked me to teach the viewers how they could do the same.

I looked at the agenda and noted that I was scheduled in along with four other speakers.

I shared the online webinar link on Facebook and Darrell decided to tune in.

"Hey guys, Mahfuz here from Candybox Marketing." I proudly announced as the webinar started.

After all five of us wrapped up our webinars, the viewers had the opportunity to rate each speaker and provide feedback. I was thrilled to see that my presentation was voted as the best webinar in the event.

I instantly received a message from Darrell: "I am super impressed by your presentation skills. You will represent our brand well!" This made me recall Brendan's advice.

The first day of work was around the corner and I looked forward to continue making a good impression. To promote our monthly workshop, I attended a networking event that was being held at a local wings restaurant.

As I took the city bus there, my heart started jumping. This reminded me of the same feeling I got before delivering my first presentation for STEPs. I put on my headphones and started playing high energy songs to pump myself up.

The bus dropped me off right in front of the restaurant and I gave myself a final pep talk before stepping in. I felt the energy as I walked through the doors. The networking had already kicked off and it made me eager to participate. I immediately engaged as many people as I could and enjoyed learning about their businesses. Although many business owners came out to promote their services, you could tell that they really wanted to create connections. They were all very pleasant and we continued exchanging business cards.

After the event ended, I jumped back on a bus and started heading home. I felt really good about the event and was excited by the idea of filling up our workshops with hundreds of business owners.

I spent the next morning sitting in my living room, pouring out all the business cards that I collected the previous night.

The follow-up process was tedious, but I knew it was necessary. I sent out dozens of emails and kept refreshing my inbox, anxiously waiting to hear back from someone.

An hour later, responses started flooding in:

"Sorry. This isn't for me."

"I don't need social media services at the moment."

"The internet is overrated and killing your generation." (Yes, this was a real message)

Although one attendee ended up signing up for the workshop, I was completely bummed out. It wasn't easy accepting all the rejections.

Darrell called me and was excited to hear about my first networking event. I told him about the devastating results and we decided to meet for coffee to chat further.

> I don't know how you do it. It felt like no one at the event had any interest in doing anything except helping themselves. Maybe we are overcharging for the workshops.

> Let me share something with you: in the early 90s, Lexus released their LS400 model and made it so affordable that Lexus drivers were furious. They didn't like the idea of this model making the brand feel 'cheap'. Lexus has created a brand so valuable, that people are happy to pay good money for it. You did amazing things with Project Reinvention and you are providing incredible value by showing business how to do this during the workshops. Once they understand your value, they will pay good money for it.

This really opened my eyes. I was starting to understand the importance of communicating self-value.

Darrell shared a few more ideas and I was beyond inspired. I appreciated that he didn't give up on me after my first failure. I told him that I wanted to keep improving myself.

"I'll tell you what I will do," he continued. "I will start taking you to my sales meetings so you can see how I do it."

He was taking me under his wing. I really wanted to continue to learn and knew that Darrell would be an ideal mentor.

"Thanks for everything, Darrell," I said as we exchanged goodbyes. I wanted to make sure that he knew how much I meant it.

The next day, I received a call from the office of Sheridan College.

"Hey Mahfuz, can you come back to the campus next week? We are doing some rebranding and everyone agrees that you have been an incredible ambassador for our college."

I wasn't sure what that meant but appreciated the compliment.

"I don't think you understand, we want you to be the new face of Sheridan College!"

CHAPTER 11

FACE OFF

"The face of Sheridan College."

It had a nice ring to it.

I searched through my closet as I tried to figure out the best outfit for the photo shoot. With limited options, I selected a striped dark blue dress shirt and the same bright red tie that I wore during my STEPs presentation. I figured the tie would bring back the good luck. Knowing that the whole city might see this, I made sure that my beard was neatly trimmed.

As I arrived on the campus, I was flabbergasted by how many other students were preparing themselves for the photo shoot. All the girls were gorgeous and the guys were much better dressed than I was.

My hopes for being the 'showcased face' quickly faded away.

"Everyone must have received the same phone call that I did," my mental chatterbox made an appearance. "What chance do I have against this great looking group?"

If there was one thing I learned by now, it was that the chatterbox could be proven wrong.

I went ahead with the photo shoot and shared a few laughs with the photographer. He shared some of the photos with me and I was pleased with the results. If I didn't make it on the college ads, at least I had some great photos to use in the future.

On my way back home, I received a call from Stephanie, my classmate from the co-op program.

> Hey, you are working for a marketing firm, aren't you?

> Yea, it has been pretty adventurous.

> I bet! I spoke to my boss at Scotiabank and he said that they were planning to roll out a new strategy using Facebook. I highly recommended you and Darrell. He wants to meet you guys tomorrow.

This was the best news I heard all day. I immediately called Darrell and he shared the excitement. We confirmed timings and I thanked Stephanie for looking out for me.

"Hey, what are friends for?" she laughed.

The next morning, I quickly changed to meet up with Darrell at Starbucks for a quick chat before we drove to the Scotiabank office, in the heart of Toronto. Trying to be on schedule, I rushed out so quickly that I put no thought to my outfit for the day.

As we prepared to start the trip, Darrell looked down and taught me a much needed lesson.

"Mahfuz, I want to thank you for setting up this meeting. As a result, I am going to give you a gift and a lesson."

I wasn't sure how to react.

"First, the lesson; we talked about sharing value with others," Darrell explained. "Part of it involves your physical appearance. We are about to meet a big executive on the top floor of one of the most established banks in the world and you decided to put on dirty running shoes."

I looked down and was immediately embarrassed by my choice of footwear. This was a valuable lesson. In our last meeting, I asked Darrell to help me improve. This meant accepting the ugly truth. In this case, the truth was just as ugly as my messy shoes.

"Now here's the gift," he continued. "As a thank you, I am going to take you next door and buy you a brand new pair of dress shoes."

We went to a classy shoe store next door and Darrell generously offered to pay for any pair of my choice. For a student struggling to pay off his debts, this was truly a gift. However, the bigger gift was the lesson I learned about the importance of demonstrating value through appearance.

We arrived at the bank's head office and checked in at the lobby.

"I will introduce you as the intern," Darrell quickly strategized. "Don't feel the pressure to contribute to the meeting. Just sit back and enjoy the show."

I reminded myself that my purpose was to learn from Darrell. I wouldn't speak, but I would definitely listen.

Stephanie welcomed us and took us up to the office. We were then greeted by their charismatic marketing manager.

Darrell stuck with the plan and introduced me as Candybox's newest intern and gave me the opportunity to sit down and take mental notes.

Within the first few minutes of the meeting, I was blown away by how Darrell conducted himself. He had the whole room laughing with his small talk and then smoothly transitioned into a business presentation. His presentation was not overly formal, but would get the right messages across through casual conversation. Darrell said all the right things to share the value of Candybox. He had great ideas and he shared it with confidence. Whatever room he was in, he owned it.

Darrell was a natural.

I learned more by being a spectator in his meetings than I could ever learn in a classroom setting. Darrell was the type of mentor that could fast-forward anyone's growth. I couldn't wait to play in the big leagues.

"That was amazing!" I said excitedly on the drive back from the meeting. "I learned so much just by being there."

Darrell smiled from the driver seat: "you will get a hang of it in no time."

I was anxious to get a shot to do what Darrell did. Similarly to public speaking, I knew this was an art I would need to master. Only time would tell.

It didn't end up taking much time as we were given a second opportunity, thanks to Ashley, another fellow classmate.

> My HVAC company is looking to redo their website and I immediately thought of you. Can Candybox help?

> When can we come in?

Darrell was so impressed by all the leads I was bringing in that he decided to take a chance on me.

"How would you like to lead this project?" Darrell invited. "It would be a great way to get your feet wet."

Opportunity of a lifetime.

I knew that some recalibration was needed. Thinking back to the meetings I attended with Darrell, I realized that I was always perceived as the student in the room. It would be very difficult to get any ideas across if they didn't see me as a marketing professional.

"You have a lot of great ideas," Darrell said with encouragement. "Communicate it with confidence."

Shifting this mindset was crucial to my success. Acting like a professional was not enough; I truly needed to believe it.

We met Ashley at her office and were introduced to the CEO of the company. I firmly shook his hand and we kicked off the meeting.

Darrell started the meeting and then gave me the opportunity to share some ideas.

Using what I learned through my public speaking experience, I pitched our plan and communicated with full confidence.

Ashley and the CEO enjoyed the pitch and immediately got on board. Candybox was hired to rebuild the company's website, drive traffic through online advertising, and design ads for bus stops and billboards.

The opportunity didn't end there. Darrell assigned this account to me and allowed me to manage my first ever project. I was honoured.

Like any millennial, I immediately pulled out my phone to share the good news with friends and family. Before I could start typing, I was caught off guard by the amount of unread messages waiting for me.

"Almost got into an accident trying to take this photo," read one of the messages.

My heart stopped after I clicked on a photo and was greeted by a 14-foot Sheridan College billboard with my face on it.

Oh My God!

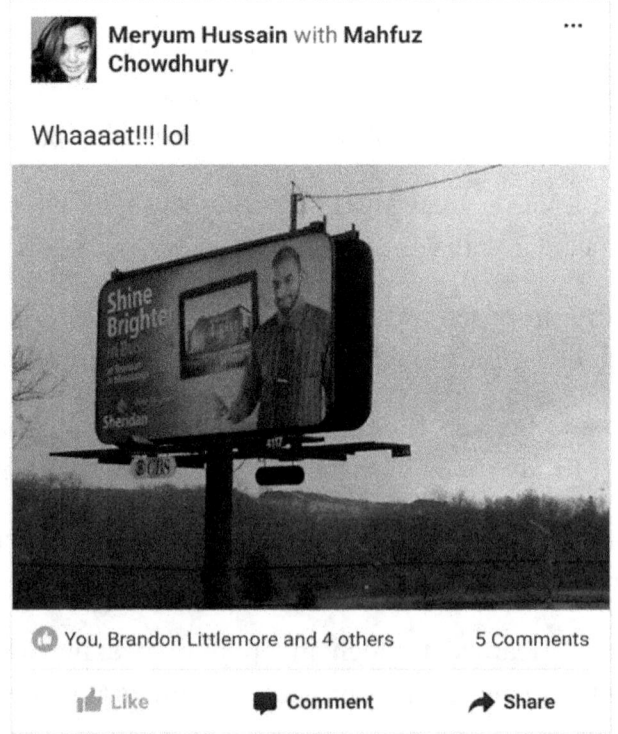

CHAPTER 12

SHOW TIME

The billboard was only the beginning. I found myself on bus stops, mall ads, newspapers, and was featured throughout Sheridan College's website.

"The kid from the coffee shop made it!" Brendan proudly announced after coming across one of the advertisements.

Everything was changing so quickly that I barely had time to review my progress. It almost felt like a decade ago since I was moping to Mike about a girl that broke my heart. It's amazing to see how much a season of reinventing can impact someone's life. I jumped back into school to resume my education, started an initiative that blew up in a few days, spoke at more events than I could keep track of, had my face greeting the city through a billboard, and was working at a company I loved. Once I hit the ground running I didn't know how to stop.

There was only a few weeks left in my work term with Candybox. I enjoyed every minute of it and knew it wasn't going to be easy saying goodbye. It was bittersweet, since I also looked forward to going back to school and focus on using the momentum to grow Project Reinvention. I got a taste of every side of the business and was excited to use the experience to improve my website's results.

That morning gave me a final taste when I opened my laptop to find a pleasant email from Darrell.

> How would you like to be on live TV? 😌
>
> I have a feeling you are about to blow my mind!

Rogers TV reached out to Candybox to do a segment about social media. They looked around for credible agencies and selected us as the ideal guests. Darrell suggested that I would be the best fit for this.

Best Internship Ever!

The night before my TV appearance, I brainstormed some ideas to discuss during the episode. Instead of getting good sleep, I spent the night navigating through YouTube, trying to find examples of entrepreneurs who gave good interviews. I took note on a lot of the attractive traits: speak slowly, long pauses, sit up straight, avoid dragging on. Feeling good about my game plan, I called it a night and managed to get less than two hours of sleep.

The next morning, I arrived at the studio and instantly started to break a sweat. You would think I'd be over the nerves after all the public speaking experience, but I needed to accept that it would always be a part of me. Trying to build excitement, I posted on Facebook and Twitter to encourage people to tune in. My mom got so excited that she relearned how to use the VCR (yes, she owns one of these) so that she could record the episode and share it with everyone.

I walked in and spotted a very energetic host who didn't waste any time sharing that she was a hugger.

"We are going to have a lot of fun!" She said enthusiastically.

I was introduced to Dave, another guest that would also be joining the panel. Dave was the owner of another marketing firm and was also invited as a guest for the episode.

The sweat was nothing compared to the feeling I got as I walked into the studio. Their professional set was filled with a camera team that was prepared to film in multiple angles. The producer was everything you would expect from Hollywood. He showed off his big personality as he walked around speaking in his headset.

They asked me to take a seat on the panel but I quickly excused myself by asking for directions to the nearest washroom. I stormed in and stared at myself in the mirror, feeling like I was going to throw up. I started thinking back to the YouTube videos I watched the previous night.

I replayed the best moments from each video and prepared myself to dive back in. I wiped the sweat down and straightened my shirt.

"This is just like any other event," I tried to remind myself. "Make Candybox proud."

I walked back in, acting like I wasn't about to self-destruct a minute ago. They attached a microphone to my shirt and guided me to my seat. The show was about to begin.

The host of the episode started by sharing a monologue about social media and then introduced Dave and myself. Within the first two minutes, Dave completely took over the interview. He would be the first one to jump in on every question and before I knew it, the first commercial break was announced before I even got a few sentences in.

"Sorry for running the show," Dave chuckled during the commercial break.

Darrell, my friends, and families were all tuning in and I was completely bombing. I needed a new strategy.

As the commercials were coming to an end, I made it a goal to get my say in every question. Dave spoke more that I did, but I spent the time giving great answers. It didn't take long before the host became so intrigued by my responses that she started focusing most of the questions towards me.

It was time for the 'viewer questions' segment. Viewers were encouraged to call in and ask us questions live on air. It was strange hearing the callers' mysterious voices coming out of the ceiling speakers.

"I am having problems with stalkers," Ashley, one of the callers started. "Creepy guys from different countries keep messaging me and going through my photos. How do I deal with this?"

Dave immediately jumped in: "You need to change your privacy settings to stop them from finding your photos." For once, I was happy he beat me to it. I needed the time to think of a more creative answer.

"Well Ashley," I started after Dave. "You are going through a problem that only a small percent of the population is going through: you are probably attractive. Get over it."

Ashley laughed on the phone and I could hear the host nervously chuckling along. She immediately asked to take a commercial break and I started to panic. I felt like I dropped the ball with such a blunt answer.

During the commercial break, the producer approached the panel and I prepared myself for a verbal spanking.

"What you just did there," he said with a smile. "Do more of it. This is what makes good TV."

I was amused and felt comfortable for the remainder of the episode.

Messages started pouring in from friends and family.

"I was so proud of how you muscled your way into each question. Your answers were great!" Darrell texted.

The episode did so well that the producer quickly invited me back to do another segment.

"Another item off my bucket list," I thought on my way home.

My work term was coming to an end but I wanted to have one more conversation with Darrell. He needed to know how much this experience helped me.

> I really wanted to thank you for everything you did for me. This work term was everything I hoped it would be and then some. You are an incredible mentor.

You earned it my friend. You put in the work.

> It's easy to work towards something you are passionate about.

So, what are your plans for the future?

> Well.. Hopefully working full-time at Candybox 😊

Mahfuz Chowdhury

Mom finds out that I am on TV so she rushes home from work, uses her limited techy skills to figure out the VCR, and proudly managed to tape the episode on VHS! Best. Mom. Ever.

👍 Gursh Sagoo and 89 others   18 Comments

 Like    Comment    Share

CHAPTER 13

DRIVEN

"How would you like to continue working for us?"

I was very pleased when Darrell gave me the opportunity to work for Candybox, on a part-time basis, while completing my final semester at school.

This wasn't easy. I would often excuse myself, during classes, to answer client phone calls in the hallway. It also required sacrificing many evenings, but I loved what I did and knew it would be worth it.

The grind wasn't going unnoticed. Jenny, from the co-op department, reached out to me and wanted to share my accomplishments with the entire country.

> We would love to nominate you for the National Co-op student of the Year Award!

> I don't even know what to say. It would be an honour.

Jenny and I spent the next few days putting together a submission and sharing my story. I had been spending a lot of time evaluating my progress so I knew exactly what I wanted to include in the biography.

Opening a blank document, I started writing about the last three years and Project Reinvention. I shared how the experience allowed me to thrive and provide great value for Candybox. There was no doubt that I would be competing with a lot of talented students, but I was confident that this story would sell itself.

Over the next few weeks, I waited anxiously for the good news. I was even more excited when Jenny announced that I would be the first Sheridan College student to ever win this award. Her support was greatly appreciated.

A few weeks later, I received a pleasant email, from the Canadian Association for Coop Education (CAFCE), congratulating me for being selected as Canada's Co-op Student of the Year.

I was speechless.

The email continued explaining how it came down to 32 finalists and that my achievement deserved the recognition for 'making a significant impact in your co-op placement and making a difference in your community'.

I was honoured.

After CAFCE published a press release, I was overwhelmed by the amount of media attention I received. My cell phone quickly used up its minutes as a result of all the interviews I did with different publications. Toronto Star, Celebrating Success Magazine, City TV, you name it. I was finally playing in the big leagues.

The next morning, I appeared on front page of our city's newspaper and couldn't be more thrilled!

"We are very pleased to announce that our very own team member, Mahfuz Chowdhury, has been named as the winner of the 2012 CAFCE Co-op Student of the Year Award!" Darrell shared on the Candybox website.

"Could not happen to a more deserving candidate. Well done Mahfuz!" Bill, the dean of Sheridan's business program, tweeted.

Messages kept flying in as the news hit the streets. Everyone continued sharing their congratulations.

"I could never look my mother in the eye and tell her that I'm giving up on her".

I thought back to a statement I made in my very first seminar. I hoped my mom was proud.

While receiving a great deal of attention, Darrell did not hesitate to offer me a full-time position at Candybox. The starting pay made any of my previous jobs look like pennies.

"All the pieces were starting to fall in place." I texted Mike about the start of my new career.

Mike also landed himself a well paying position at Ford Motors and was now engaged to Jeannine, a great girl he met from work whom he was deeply in love with. I couldn't be prouder of him.

This called for a celebration.

> I want you to help me pick out a graduation gift.

> For sure! What did you have in mind?

> Well, I am sure you are sick of driving me around. And I'm definitely sick of travelling around in a bus.
>
> Are you saying what I think you are saying?
>
> It's time to treat myself to a brand new car!

"I feel like getting a sports car." I felt like spoiling myself.

The sports car that won my heart was the brand new Scion FR-S that was going to be released for the first time by Toyota and Subaru.

"Alexis," I decided to name her. "It meant: helper and defender." It seemed fitting as Project Reinvention had the same purpose.

After a quick test drive, I immediately signed on the dotted line.

Shortly after, Mike got himself a gorgeous new Ford Mustang. We wasted no time setting up a professional photo shoot with our new ladies.

As we reviewed the photos, Mike and I reflected on how far we came from serving coffee at Tim Horton's. All we had was a visor and a dream.

"We both had the drive to win," I said during the fancy car photo shoot, hoping he would catch the pun. "We made all this happen."

That night, I laid in my bed, finding it extremely hard falling asleep. The adrenaline was running through my veins in excitement.

I thought about all the different areas of my life and how I started to gain control.

"Fear and stress is a result of not having control of a situation," a valuable lesson Darrell taught me.

At that moment, I realized that there was still one part of my life I did not have under control. It was something I should have sorted out years ago. It was a feeling that left a nasty hole through my heart.

It was time to make things right with my ex girlfriend.

CHAPTER 14

SHOEBOX

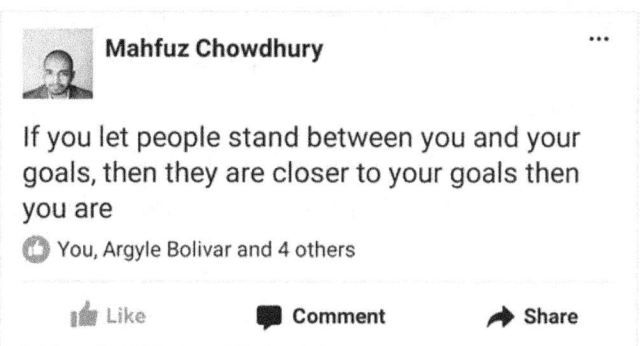

"I need to get this under control."

This was the first topic of our conversation as Mike and I met up the following week.

It's been almost five years since she's been in my life but I can't deny that the chip on my shoulder stayed with me. I've been in several shorter relationships since being with her, and most of them came to a bitter end as a result of my trust issues. I found it virtually impossible to trust someone after getting burned.

> You got every other part of your life handled. You need to figure out a way to get this sorted out.

> I have actually been thinking about it for a while. I think I'm going to get back in touch with my ex.

> What are you going to say?

> I don't know. I'll figure it out along the way. We never got closure after the messy breakup and I wanted to make things right.

It was time to make amends. I no longer held a grudge against her. It was time to accept the fact that our relationship was already on rocky grounds. We were arguing every single day and I lost my temper far too often. If I didn't end the relationship at that moment, it would've likely destructed naturally.

I started to question if I was simply a terrible boyfriend. She was amazing for most of our relationship and I might have taken it for granted.

I didn't know what I was going to say; I just wanted us to be in good terms.

That night, I looked up her contact information and started to hesitate. What if she moved on with her life? What if she wanted nothing to do with me? I decided that I would leave it up to her.

"Hey," I started writing. "I know it's been many years since we spoke. I've been doing a lot of reflecting lately and you came to mind. I just wanted you to know that you have been a big part of my life and I hate the way things ended. At the end of it all, I want us to at least be friends. I would love to meet in person just to chat and catch up."

Hour after hour, I would keep checking my phone for a response, only to be left disappointed. Her silence was so loud that I could hear it clearly. She had moved on and I would have to accept that.

I went for a long drive to clear my head. Things are going so good in my life so I couldn't figure out why it bothered me that much. I reminded myself: part of personal growth means letting go of the things holding you back.

"When you are holding a grudge," a speaker once said at a seminar, "you are drinking the poison and hoping it will kill them." I chuckled while thinking about the analogy. After much pondering, I decided it was time to drive home and call it a night.

The next morning, a message appeared on my phone that resurrected hope back in me.

> Sorry, I needed time to think. It's been like five years! I wasn't sure what to say. Is this really how you feel?

> A hundred percent. I don't have any expectations and don't want to put any pressure on you. I just want to make things right.

> Alright. So when did you want to meet?

> What are you doing for lunch?

We made plans and I offered to pick her up from apartment. She responded back by sending an attachment with a message attached: "I held on to this for years. I just couldn't throw it out."

I opened up the attachment and saw a photograph of a shelf that consisted of all the gifts I have given her throughout our relationship. Everything from the first necklace to the Raptor stuffed animal that I bought after our first Toronto Raptors game.

"So you have your very own Mahfuz shrine, huh?" I joked, trying not to act like I was absolutely blown away.

I drove up to her apartment and she was already waiting in the lobby. She still looked as gorgeous as the first time I met her.

"I love your car! Can I keep it?" she said with a laugh as she stepped in.

We hugged tightly. This immediately gave me flashbacks to the day she threw her arms around my neck crying. I broke away from the memory and started driving.

I suggested chatting over Starbucks so that I could get my caffeine fix. Once we arrived, she sat in a corner table and smiled in my direction while I picked up our drink orders and walked back to her table.

> You look amazing!
>
> Took the words right out of my mouth.
>
> Still the super charming Mahfuz, huh?

We spend hours catching up before she hit me with: "I have to show you something."

I watched curiously as she reached in her large purse and pulled out a giant shoebox. The shoebox was fully decorated with art and photographs. The side of the box wrote 'M ❤ T' with a fun border around it.

"I made this memory box when we were dating," she said with a smile. "I held on to everything you ever gave me."

I braced myself as she walked me through memory lane.

She proceeded to take everything out of the box and took her time to show and tell.

I spent so much time dwelling on the way we ended our relationship that I forgot about the good moments. She pulled out all the handwritten notes I would leave in her locker, along with a handful of smaller gifts that I gave her. She also reminded me of all the bigger ones that was still sitting on her shelf.

Staring in disbelief, I instantly felt my doubts about being a terrible boyfriend flush out of my head. I read through the letters and remembered how I treated her like an angel. Everything in that box proved how often I would go over and beyond for her.

This was the reassurance I needed.

She was impressed by how well things were going in my life.

> I keep seeing your face everywhere! You have become a celebrity.
>
> Watch out now, you are one compliment away from making my head explode with over confidence.
>
> Lol! Seriously though, I know how hard things were for you. I am so proud of how much you have turned things around.
>
> Stop it, I'm blushing 😊

After many fun conversations, I dropped her back to her house and hugged her one last time.

"Thank you," I said as she started stepping out of the car. "Not just for making amends, but also helping me move on with my life."

On my drive home, something felt very different. I was feeling something that I haven't felt before.

Revisiting our best memories and being back in good terms allowed me to get the closure I was aching for a very long time. The devil of doubt had left my shoulders.

I was ready to trust again.

CHAPTER 15

GLORIOUS GENTLEMEN

My new-found trust would soon be tested when I was invited to go out with a group of strangers.

Mike and I were well known for surrounding ourselves with a small group of trustworthy friends. I always hesitated before letting new people enter my circle.

It was especially difficult when my infamous chatterbox came back to life:

"These guys will try to use you."

Knowing that I needed to get out of my comfort zone and silence my inner talk, I accepted the invitation.

I walked into a stranger's house and immediately felt the anxiety of being in an unfamiliar territory. Seeing a group of guys laughing in the living room, I thought it would be polite to introduce myself.

"I'm Kamil," said a tall bald guy as he stood up. "Welcome to my house!"

I looked around the room to see a series of guitars hanging on the wall. I admired Kamil's love for music. What was more admirable was Kamil's desire to learn. I knew we would get along as soon as we started discussing psychology and how the human mind works. Kamil would later tell me that he wanted to get into the field of medicine and I had no doubt someone as smart as he was could pull it off.

"Romulo, nice to meet you" said the quieter one in the room.

It didn't take long before I realized how much thrill Romulo found in different areas of life, whether it was competitive gaming, skateboarding, or pursuing a career as a police officer. He mentioned that he was currently working as a security guard and I encouraged him to take the next step.

"Hey man, I'm Jorge," said the shorter one with a smile.

Jorge and I briefly met at Sheridan College around the same time I started Project Reinvention. It was comforting to meet someone I recognized in the room.

Jorge had a passion for media arts and making videos. It was easy to see how much he loved it when he would share film ideas or criticize movies we would watch.

"Hi, I'm Brown." said the fourth person that stood up.

"Me too" I said with a smile as the rest of the room laughed.

His name was Michael but he preferred to be called Brown. Brown was the upbeat one in the room. His positive energy would quickly make him the life of any party. Brown had a passion to become a child youth worker. With that type of energy, that would have been my first guess.

I was later introduced to the five other members of their group. All of them had their own set of goals and it was amazing seeing them all work together to achieve them. They mentioned that most of them had been friends since high school and I could tell they really trusted one another. It reminded me of my friendship with Mike.

After introductions and small talks, we decided to go out to a local pub. It was amazing to see how many different personalities quickly bonded. I don't think I have ever met a group that was so genuine and trustworthy. This was very rare and extremely refreshing.

Since that night, we would regularly make plans to explore everything that our city had to offer. Whether it was rocking out at karaoke nights, exchanging gifts during Secret Santa, or flying out to Dominican for vacation, every moment with this group made me forget about any problems in my life.

The group evolved each month and I always appreciated how often we would encourage each other to move closer to our goals. We would even host yearly award shows to reward each person for their contribution to the group. It was like our very own Grammys (yes, we all did live performances. No, it wasn't any good).

I knew that hashing things out with my ex would bring trust back into my life. I just had no idea that it would work itself out that quickly.

This group would have never been a chapter in my life if I didn't accept the invitation at Kamil's house. Life can pleasantly surprise you with every decision you make.

I learned how important it was to get out of my comfort zone in order to truly reinvent myself. I understood that change was uncomfortable at first, but if I was willing to step out of the box it would eventually become part of my comfort zone.

I owed it to these incredible gentlemen for the healthy reminder. I was honoured to be included in their glorious circle.

One night, Kamil and I got together and engaged in a deep conversation. The conversation left us both inspired.

> We should write a book together.

> What would we write about?

That was a question I asked myself multiple times.

Since that conversation, my mind continued drifting back to the idea of sharing value through a published book.

"Do I write a book about marketing or about personal development?" I wondered every time I opened a fresh Word document. I was passionate about both and had enough information to discuss either subject.

After much debate, I decided to focus on providing value through my personal story. Instead of writing a marketing book, I was going to write a book about a millennial who just happens to be working in the field of marketing.

I thanked Kamil for sparking the idea in my brain and allowed me to take on a new challenge.

Admittedly, no matter how many times I tried writing, I kept calling it quits when I couldn't determine how to conclude the book.

I stopped writing. I decided that I wasn't ready.

I had a strange feeling that there were a few more chapters left in this journey.

CHAPTER 16

BEST MAN

"We need to talk."

You never know whether to expect good news or bad news when receiving a message like this.

Mike sent it one morning as I was settling in to my new full time position. We decided to meet for coffee and chat since this seemed like something he wanted to discuss in person.

I stepped into our meeting spot, still not sure what to expect.

Mike arrived on schedule and greeted me with a smile. Fortunately, his smile was a sign of good news to come.

> We've grown up together and have come a long way.

> It truly is amazing to see how far we have come.

> I've had many challenges and doubts in my life, but one thing I never doubted was your friendship and loyalty. You always had my back.

Mike handed me a DVD of one of our favourite comedies, Hangover 2, and it had a note wrapped around it. I took a closer look:

"We met 10 years ago & we've been best friends since," the note read. "From getting jacked together at Planet Workout to Wonderland trips to Timmies drama to indoor soccer championships. We went through it all and I couldn't think of anyone else that would be more worthy of being the best man at my wedding. Will you join my Wolf Pack as my BEST MAN?"

I was truly honoured.

With no hesitation, I graciously accepted. Mike was single-handedly responsible for helping me get back up on my feet during the most difficult phase of my life. I would often tell people the importance of surrounding themselves with quality people instead of simply trying to become popular. One amazing friend could spark the inspiration you need to achieve anything in the world. I knew with full certainty, Mike was that amazing friend.

The date he selected for the wedding worked well since it was exactly one day before I would attend my older brother's wedding reception. It was going to be an eventful weekend.

Mike also mentioned that he was in search of someone who could film the wedding. I immediately thought of Jorge and highly recommended him.

After heading home from the celebration, I started to put some time into writing the best man speech. Although I could go on and on about how great Mike is, I found it very difficult to summarize it within one speech.

No matter how many presentations I have put together, throughout my public speaking adventures, this was becoming the most challenging. Mike has done so much for me over the years. Where do I start?

During the bachelor party and our regular hangouts, I would act confident and at ease. However, a part of me was in constant panic as this was a really big deal. I needed to nail this speech.

Similarly to the preparation I did for my Rogers TV appearance, I watched YouTube clips of different best man speeches but was discouraged as most of them showed the speakers crash and burning. This preparation ritual only made me panic.

I remembered that Brendan recently delivered a best man speech so I reached out to him for some advice. He shared his speech with me and provided pointers.

"Let me know when you're doing yours," Brendan said excitedly. "I'd definitely like to give it a listen!"

With the wedding date coming up, I spent a series of late nights brainstorming and rehearsing the speech.

It soon became a masterpiece. I felt great about it and looked forward to Mike's big day.

Let the wedding bells ring.

I walked into the church and greeted Jorge as he was setting up his camera on wedding day. It was show time.

I stood on stage, with the biggest smile, as Mike and Jeannine exchanged vows on their wedding day. It only took a glimpse of those two before you knew how crazy they were for each other.

It was time to relocate. The bridesmaid and groomsmen got into the limo as we made our way down to the reception after a brief photo shoot. While on route, we all raised a glass for Mike and Jeannine and looked forward to an entertaining evening.

With minutes to go before my speech, I chugged my glass of ice water and mentally rehearsed one final time before standing behind the podium.

"I would like to say how privileged I am to be Mike's best man on his very special day," I started. "Thank you Mike. More importantly, I really appreciate that you and Jeannine dressed up so nicely for my special occasion." The crowd laughed and, like every talk I had ever done, the laughs immediately put me at ease.

I went on to share humorous moments that I witnessed during the evolution of Mike's relationship with Jeannine. I acknowledged how proud I was to see Mike marry someone as caring, warm and loving as Jeannine.

I finished the speech with one final note:

"Mike, over the last ten years we have witnessed each other go through the highest highs and lowest lows of our lives. There were days that we felt like we hit rock bottom, and I will never forget our conversations about how we will bounce back and sit on top of the world. We knew it wouldn't be easy, but we knew it would be worth it."

After a short pause, I continued.

"Throughout my life, I have met people that motivated me, people that entertained me, people that challenged me, and people that inspired me. And Mike, you are the only person I have ever met that did all of the above. You are my best friend, my brother, and someone I will always look up to."

I made a final toast and Mike stood up to thank me for the speech.

"You hit me in the feels with that last part," Mike said with a chuckle.

I put my speech away and sat down in relief as the worrying was over. It was time to party with the guests.

The entire wedding was flawless; everything from the amazing speeches to Mike and I break dancing in the middle of the venue. Mike and Jeannine had completely outdone themselves.

At a certain point during the night, I took a seat to give my feet a well-deserved break. I looked around the room and was fascinated by all the joy.

Seeing Mike and Jeannine dancing at the center of the room made me think about how much I missed being in love.

I thought about how my future wife was out there somewhere, going through her own adventures and pursuing her passion. I loved the idea of sharing the dance floor with her one day.

I couldn't wait to meet her.

After an amazing night, I woke up the next morning and immediately remembered that I had a second event to attend. I wished Mike and Jeannine an incredible honeymoon and then changed into another suit to make way down to my brother's wedding.

I arrived in a great mood after thinking about the epic celebration from the previous night. Being slightly late, I quickly walked in and started shaking hands with family and friends who were excited to see me.

Going from a Canadian-Portuguese reception to a Bengali one was a big transition, but equally as enjoyable.

After taking my seat at the front of the room, I looked up at the beautiful crowd. I was excited to meet all the new friends that joined us for this celebration.

Never would I have expected my future fiancé to be sitting in this room.

CHAPTER 17

MONDAY MORNINGS

Both weddings were a big success and it was time to get back on the grind.

Candybox Marketing wasted no time picking up pace as we continued growing each year.

Our team now consisted of seven members and a few talented interns that we hired through our relationship with Sheridan College.

The next few months got more exhilarating as I travelled to several cities in Ontario for Candybox's first ever Social Media Tour.

This involved us speaking at fourteen cities over the course of four weeks. I wasn't a great singer so this was the closest I would ever be to living the life of a rock star.

We decided it was a good time to get ourselves an office for client meetings and team collaborations.

"I don't want us to think of it as an office," Darrell announce during a team meeting. "Let's call it a 'studio'. If I ever call it an office I owe you all coffee."

It wasn't just the name. It was the lifestyle.

Darrell shared his vision about how he wanted to move away from the typical offices we would find in most corporate environments.

Instead of working out of cubicles, we created an open concept atmosphere so that our team members could interact. Darrell purchased three large tables, that were custom made with fine dark wood, and placed them at the center of the room. We then added chairs around the tables to allow the team to sit wherever they wanted. Maybe it was our countless Starbucks visits that inspired this, but it definitely created a healthier culture.

Our team members had the option to work from home or to come in to the studio, based on their preferences. We would also decorate the studio with superhero posters and figures, along with other additions that our team brought from home. Our studio was ready.

I always loved the idea of doing things differently. It made it easy to keep our creative juices flowing.

By this period, I found myself managing dozens of website projects at a time. Our team was expanding, the number of website projects was growing, and my responsibilities were increasing. One thing that hadn't changed was my passion for growing the business and my love for Marketing.

"How does Darrell manage to keep you around?" Jenny one day asked me while catching up over lunch.

It was a great question and one that I knew exactly how to answer.

"I remember that feeling of hating Monday mornings," I explained. "It's not easy getting out of bed when you had to get up and do things you didn't want to do.

I loved what I did every day and Darrell always found a way to keep me challenged. No two days were ever the same."

It was amazing being a part of a company whose accomplishments weren't going unnoticed. Our team's incredible work gained a lot of recognition and was often used as a case story in business classes.

Mondays were about to get even better when I received an early morning email from someone new. For the purpose of this book, I will call her Ayesha:

"Hey! This is a bit random but I am a friend of your sister-in-law and saw you at your brother's wedding. We talked about you for a while and I thought I would send you a message and say hi."

Ayesha and I never had the pleasure of meeting during my brother's wedding so I figured it would be nice to meet up with someone who took the time out to write me an email.

I wrote back and we decided to meet at a restaurant in North York to chat over delicious crepes.

Knowing how overly formal first meetings can be, I decided to dress casual with a t-shirt, jeans, and a baseball cap.

Upon arriving at the location, I was speechless when I noticed a gorgeous girl step in with long black hair and perfect olive skin. I greeted and pulled a chair out for her, hoping to demonstrate chivalry.

We immediately hit it off.

> When I saw you at the wedding, I was so impressed by how charming you were when you walked around and shook hands. I asked your sister-in-law about you and she said you were single.

> My skin tone doesn't show it, but I am definitely blushing.

> Well, blushing or not, I think you are very handsome.

> You are not bad yourself. An easy 6.5 out of 10 😊

We flirted for a bit before sharing a snapshot of our lives. Ayesha worked as a teller at a local bank and was going to school to become a dental hygienist.

I couldn't get over how much her love of life was oozing through every word. Her upbeat personality had my full attention and I was already hoping to see her again.

We started dating and my attraction for her started growing more each day. We would go out to board game cafes to share laughs over a competitive game of Monopoly and rub it in whenever one of our blocks collapsed during a game of Jenga. I felt at home with her.

Thinking about how my past relationships came crashing down like Jenga blocks, I wanted to do this one right. I found myself being patient and more courteous towards Ayesha. She had her group of friends and I had mine, so we would always share funny stories that happened with them throughout the week. We also worked a lot, so we gave each other respectful space to focus on our passion. We literally never fought or had heated arguments. There was never a date that wasn't fun and enjoyable.

It didn't take long before I started to feel something that I haven't felt in a very long time. I would find myself thinking about Ayesha every hour and counting down the days before I got to see her again.

No need for sugar coating: I was crazy about her. I loved her.

This might have been one of the happiest moments of my life. Whether it involved speaking at events, creating magic with the Candybox team, hanging out with close friends, or spending time with Ayesha, I couldn't wait to see what each day had in store for me.

My birthday was around the corner and Ayesha immediately booked my weekend for an exciting evening together.

We met at a famous Thai restaurant to chat and I was completely caught off guard when our server snuck up behind me with a homemade cake and candles.

"Happy birthday, old man" She said with a giggle.

I looked her in the eye and couldn't stop smiling. Baking a cake for my birthday? She was an absolute sweetheart. I tried thinking of a birthday wish but, for the first time ever, I had no idea what to wish for. Everything was going so good. Instead, I just thanked God for making all my past wishes come true and blew out the candles. We spent the remainder of the night sharing laughs and exchanging stories.

Over the next few weeks, I started thinking about starting a new chapter in my life. I thought about how most people in my life were getting married in their early 20s and having kids by the time they were my age. I was falling behind. With everything going my way, there was no better time to take the next step with the girl I loved.

I took Ayesha out to a classy sushi restaurant and prepared myself to have a life changing conversation with her. Sweating before public speaking events didn't hold a candle to how nervous I was.

We sat at a private booth and I stuttered over my words as I started telling her how much she meant to me.

"I've been doing a lot of thinking," I shared with her. "I thought a lot about what my perfect future looks like and I see you in it."

I could see the twinkle in her eyes as I slowly held her hand.

"Ayesha, will you marry me?"

CHAPTER 18

CHATTERBOX STRIKES BACK

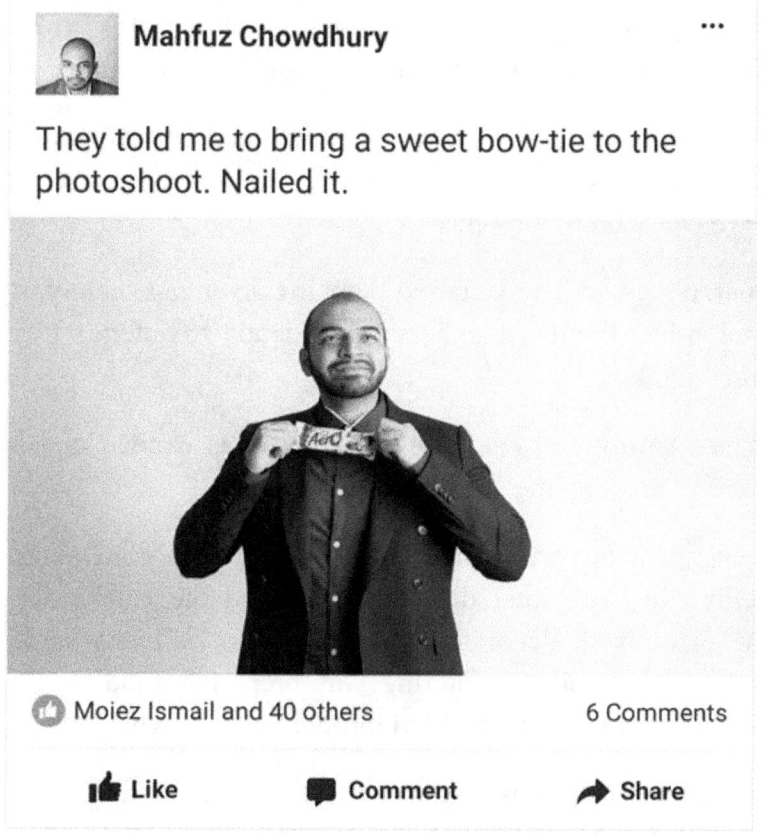

"Hey, guess what?"

This was the start of all my messages as I shared the incredible news with family and friends.

I met with Mike and wasted no time asking him to be my best man.

"I am so happy for you, man!" Mike said with joy as he attentively listened to the entire story. "I know everything you have been through and believe me when I say this: you deserve it."

"Congrats!!!" Jeannine shared the congratulations. "You honestly deserve the best and it's awesome to hear that you are finding that. She's so lucky to have snagged you!"

The Candybox team asked for full details during our next meeting and Darrell took me out to lunch to personally congratulate me.

"You have no idea how happy I am for you," Darrell said during lunch. "You have worked so hard to get to where you are and you deserve every bit of happiness."

My parents immediately started planning an engagement party and invited other family members and friends to attend. Life was moving quickly.

Ayesha's family and friends were equally as excited and looked forward to meeting me.

The engagement party planning started and family members were travelling in from long distances to attend the celebration. The house was well decorated with flowers, balloons and large 'congratulations' signs. Catering was preparing food on the side table to keep the guests well fed throughout the night.

I was asked to wait in my room until the guests settled in and Ayesha would also be isolated in another room so that we could not see each other until the reception started.

Before Ayesha arrived, I snuck in a hand-written letter to her room to read while waiting.

"You are beautiful, funny, charming, and one of the biggest dorks I know," the letter read. "I can't wait to call you my wife."

A few minutes later, Ayesha arrived with her group and was immediately escorted to a private room. She took her friends in to keep her company and I could hear the loud 'aww' from my side of the room, as her friends read the letter with her.

"Way to go, Lance Romance," I thought with a smile.

Mike and Jeannine soon arrived and were directed to my room. I thanked them for coming and we killed time discussing the events that were about to unfold that night. They continued reminding me of how happy they were for me and couldn't wait for all our future double-dates.

A knock on our door notified us that the reception was about to begin. Mike and Jeannine were guided back downstairs to join the gathering and I looked at myself in the mirror one last time to make sure everything was in place.

Music started playing as I slowly made my way down the stairs. I saw mine and Ayesha's parents waiting at the bottom of the steps and gave them all hugs as I made it down to the main floor. Waiting with excitement, I looked up the stairs to see Ayesha slowly making her way down in a gorgeous silk blue dress. She looked breathtaking.

Ayesha joined me at the main floor and we both immediately locked arms to make our way to the living room to take our special seats.

"You look beautiful," I told her as we started walking. She thanked me while blushing.

As I walked towards my seat, I looked around to see all the happy guests smiling and waving. I saw Mike and Jeannine sitting beside our designated seats. Mike gave me the thumbs up and Jeannine took photos as we walked by. The reception was going flawlessly.

I verbally welcomed all the guests as Ayesha and I took our seats. The crowd then gathered to the front of our seats and started taking so many photos that we felt like the newest Hollywood power couple.

"Brangelina has nothing on us," I thought with a smile.

The reception continued as we formally exchanged rings and took photos with everyone. I made it a goal to personally greet every single guest at the event. I stood up to work the room after the formal part of the event was finished.

I spoke with Ayesha's parents, uncles, aunts, friends, and even the little cousins who were running around playfully.

"Hey, nice suit!" I kneeled down and said to the little cousin wearing a shiny silver tuxedo. "I thought I was supposed to be the best-dressed guy here. You stole the show!" Everyone in the room laughed.

During dinner, Ayesha and I sat with Mike and Jeannine to chat. Ayesha got excited about our future.

> We need to all go out soon. I can show you some great places!

Jeannine was equally as excited.

> I was saying the same thing. Double dates will be so much fun!

Mike and I shared a few funny stories from our past and called ourselves the 'ring brothers' as we gave props with our rings and joked about how it would give us superpowers.

The night started coming to an end as all the guests were exchanging goodbyes. I was thrilled by the success of the event and felt the need to live up to my millennial name by announcing the engagement on Facebook.

My mom hugged me again and told me that she was extremely happy. My dad said he was so proud of how much I had turned my life around over the last few years. These were things I dreamed of hearing from my parents for a very long time.

It wasn't easy going to sleep with that much adrenaline pumping through my veins. I stayed up most of the night texting Ayesha about different things that happened throughout the night.

"My family and friends love you," she wrote in one of her messages. "They all couldn't believe how relaxed and confident you are. My sister said that she can tell that you would never hurt me and would always care about me."

Her sister hit it right on the nose.

I had an instant change in my mindset as my purpose was now to make Ayesha the happiest girl in the world. Every decision I would make would be to better her life.

The next few days involved celebrating with friends and other family members. I was never a great sleeper to begin with, but now I was finding it impossible. I would stay up late at nights thinking about the future and making each move with precise calculation.

I wish I could say that each late night was a result of maximum happiness but the demons in my head would make a frequent visit.

"She wasn't around in your life when things were going downhill," my negative chatterbox would say during its late night visits. "Why does she want to marry you anyway?"

Trying to focus on the positive, I would do everything I could to muzzle the negative thoughts.

"Don't mess this up, Mahfuz." I kept repeating to myself. "Everything is going so good. Please don't mess this up."

In most cases, I was able to successfully silence my inner chatterbox. This time, it won the battle after striking back with brutal force.

I started to panic and reached for my phone to chat with Ayesha.

Entering, from stage-left, the conversation that ruins my life.

CHAPTER 19

HEARTBREAK

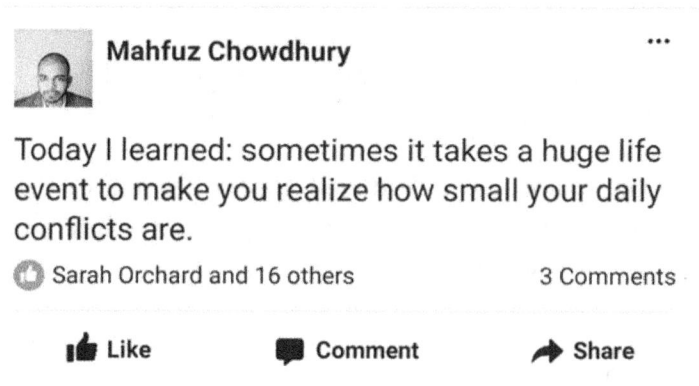

Ayesha started the conversation talking about wedding plans. I was a bit out of touch on Muslim weddings so I asked her to educate me. She spent some time explaining the different parts of the wedding, including 'Mahr', which involved a payment or possession that would be promised to be paid by the groom to the bride at the time of marriage.

This didn't bother me too much until she started dwelling about the Mahr.

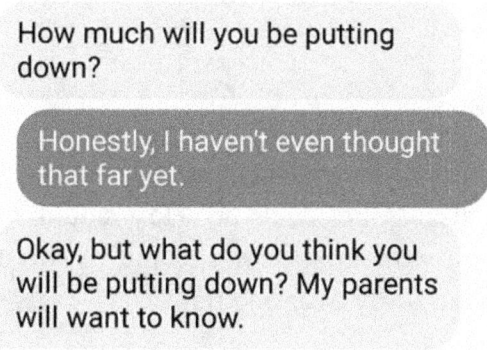

After asking me a few more times, I got irritated and the anxiety started to kick in once again.

"Why do you even love someone like me?" I said to Ayesha without even realizing how low my self-confidence was.

I wasn't prepared for the earful I would get from Ayesha.

"How could you ask that?" She said loudly. "You think I am with you because of your money?"

Frankly, I didn't think that was the case at all. I loved her and simply needed reassurance.

She lost her temper and continued yelling until she was in tears. This was actually the first time we ever got into a fight and I wasn't sure how to deal with it.

I tried to calm her down but she said she needed some time to think and then ended our conversation.

"Way to screw it up, Mahfuz." I thought to myself. I decided to respect her wishes and give her some time to think.

The next morning my dad sent me a text message that made my heart sink.

"Ayesha's parents called me and said that they want to call off the wedding. They contacted me and asked you to never contact Ayesha again."

Fuck!

I couldn't believe this was happening. Ayesha and I didn't even get the chance to discuss her decision. How could she make such a reckless decision without speaking to me? I was furious that she was throwing it all away over one fight.

Deciding to speak to my parents about it, I went to their house and got in a heated argument. I could tell that they were embarrassed by the fact that they told the world about the engagement and invited everyone to the party.

"You need to fix this. You brought shame to the family!" I knew my dad said this out of anger but it immediately made me lose my temper and snap back at him.

After cooling off in my room, I decided to go back down to the living room to talk it out but instantly broke into tears when I saw my dad laying on the floor having a heart attack.

"Look what you did!" my mom put the blame on me and I immediately fell to my lowest point.

I quickly pulled out my phone and dialed 9-1-1. Paramedics arrived within minutes and stormed through our front door to check on my dad.

I couldn't stop the tears from pouring out while watching the paramedics attach a heart monitor to my dad's chest, to assess the situation.

They reassured us that he would be fine and carried him out in a mobile bed to give him a more detailed checkup in the hospital.

I quickly jumped into my car and started following the ambulance to the emergency room. While following the ambulance, I kept hearing the echo of my mom saying "look what you did" and let out the worst cry that I had in my life.

As I arrived at the emergency room, I could see my mom and brother already in the waiting room. My brother said that they should be getting the results soon. Although we sat in silence, I knew that they blamed me for everything and I truly felt like the worst person alive.

I pulled out my phone and put my thoughts in writing, as I sent a text message to Mike:

"I ruined everything. Everything was good and I screwed everything up."

Mike asked if he could call but I knew that I couldn't answer the call in the emergency room. I told him that I would speak to him later. I didn't want to be a second away from my dad's room.

"I break everything that I touch." I thought to myself as I had flashbacks to the doors closing behind all my relationships and now putting my dad through hell.

After an hour, the doctor approached us in the hallway to inform us that my dad would be okay. The doctor mentioned that he had a few blockages and would still require surgery to reduce the chance of another heart attack.

The doctor saw me leaning against the wall in tears and pulled me aside for an explanation.

I summarized the situation and told him that I should not have lost my temper. I told him that I felt completely responsible for this. The doctor tried to put me at ease by putting his hands on my shoulder and shared his wisdom:

"I know this is going to be hard for you to accept, but it wasn't your fault. Your dad has had heart problems for a very long time and the blockages would have caused this sooner or later."

The doctor stated that the surgery would help my dad become healthier than he was before the heart attack. This was what I would continue praying for.

My dad was transferred to another wing and they started the surgery. My mom and brother waited for hours and started taking shifts to grab food or get rest. I refused to leave my post. No matter how exhausted I was, I just had to be there for my dad when the surgery was complete. I sat in the closest chair and continued praying to God to help my dad make it through this.

Hours later, one of the surgeons came out and mentioned that the surgery was a success.

Nothing I have ever accomplished in my life felt as good as hearing this news.

We were given an opportunity to see our dad before he was relocated to a more comfortable room to get rest.

I walked into the room to find my dad resting in a bed with a heart-shaped pillow lying on his chest.

I slowly approached him and could tell that he was highly medicated. My dad slightly opened his eyes and reached out for my hand. I held his hand and he squeezed back tightly.

"I am so sorry, Dad." I said with tears in my eyes. "I am so sorry."

My dad started to doze off as he slowly whispered: "We will be okay."

As the nurse started transferring him to his overnight room, she stated that one guest could stay the night to watch over him. I immediately volunteered and reminded my dad that I would be there every step of the way.

Throughout the night, my dad would wake up with excruciating back pain. I would aid him with a back massage and readjust his sleeping position to make it easier to relax.

After massaging his back, I held his hand and opened up to him in a way that I never have before.

"I love you so much dad. You have been there for me when everything was going wrong and you rooted me on when everything started going right. You never gave up on me and I want you to know that I will never give up on you. I love you, dad."

I was interrupted by loud fireworks in the background. I forgot that day was Canada Day. As my dad started to doze off, I sat on a chair and shared a genuine message with my friends:

"There is a lot to love about our country but today I couldn't be more thankful for the amazing Health Care that we are lucky to have.

My dad recently had a heart attack and had to go through an open heart surgery. The doctors said that everything went great and were able to remove all blockages in his arteries. We are now here with him as he is resting and should be ready to go home soon.

Happy Canada Day! I look forward to spending it with the strongest and most inspiring person I know."

CHAPTER 20

LIKE A CHAMPION

"I'm not ready to give up yet."

This was the mentality I had as I contacted Ayesha to meet one more time.

My dad was released from the hospital and was resting peacefully at home. I decided to now focus on righting another wrong in my life, by working things out with Ayesha.

She agreed to meet at the crepe restaurant where we first met. This location started to feel like a poetic tragedy.

I decided to meet with Mike, before seeing Ayesha, to bring him up to speed about the break up and my dad's heart attack. Mike was very empathetic but also shared some great advice.

"It's called 'cold feet' bro," he started explaining. "I know you don't know what this feels like in relationships but everyone gets this. Even I got it."

Mike always knew the right things to say at the right time.

"You did nothing wrong by asking her why she wanted to marry you," Mike continued. "Everyone needs reassurance from time to time. Jeannine always gave that reassurance to me and that's how I knew she was the right one for me."

Mike also shared the same disbelief that Ayesha would throw it all away over our first fight.

"You are both adults and you will have arguments. Couples will find ways to work it out if they truly loved each other."

Mike had a valid point. As counterintuitive as it sounds, Ayesha and I should've had at least one fight before getting engaged. I didn't know how she reacted under these circumstances and whether she would immediately walk away from the relationship.

After a lengthy pep talk with Mike, I was mentally prepared to meet Ayesha. I didn't know whether it was going to be a good meeting or not; I just knew that I was ready for either outcome.

Arriving to the restaurant before Ayesha, I knew it wasn't going to end well when she walked in with a bag full of gifts that I bought for her. I wanted her to at least see things from my perspective.

"I haven't been able to sleep properly since our last conversation," I started as we settled into our seats.

She leaned forward and gave me the opportunity to share my side of the story. This was all I really wanted.

> Ever since we got engaged, I have been sharing the news with everyone I know and talking about how amazing you are.

I have been doing that as well. My friends and family were so excited for me.

> But here lies the screw up. After sharing all the exciting news and thinking about our future, I felt a feeling that I never felt before, which Mike later told me that it was simply 'cold feet'.

I know how you feel. I was feeling the same.

> I started freaking out and panicking and this made me start acting unusual and do a lot of things I would never do.

Mahfuz, listen...

> Hang on, let me finish.

Okay, go ahead.

> I hate the way I acted because of this freak out and it made me do a lot of things that I regret. No matter what I said in our last conversation, I never questioned why you wanted to be with me because I already knew the answer through all of your actions.

> I do understand what you are saying but after everything that just happened, I don't want to go forward anymore. Everything got really ugly.

Is she serious?

As prepared as I thought I was, I felt my anger rising as she let one moment of doubt replace all our good memories.

After discussing it further for another ten minutes, I realized that this was pointless. There was no hope.

"You can keep all the gifts," I said, waving the white flag. "I bought them for you and don't plan to give it to anyone else."

I told her that spending more time wasn't going to make it any easier and decided to call the waiter for the bill.

As we walked out, I gave her a final hug.

> Are you going to be okay?

> I've hit rock bottom before. The difference is that this time I know I will bounce back.

Frankly, I wasn't sure if I actually believed it myself.

On my drive home, Mike called me and wanted to hear about how it went.

"I'm a walking time-bomb. Everything I touch I destroy." I said as Mike and I met at a local lounge. Clearly, I wasn't ready to bounce back.

Brown, Romulo, and Jorge also joined to help pick me back up to my feet.

Mike reminded me how I worked on myself to get back on top every single time something went wrong. The others encouraged me to do the same.

"Results don't lie." Mike spoke about my accomplishments. "I don't know anyone who recovered better than you. Take this as an opportunity to become selfish for once. You've earned it."

I was lucky to have the most incredible friends.

Delivering the bad news wasn't easy. I would go to work and my team members would ask whether I have set a date for the wedding. My family members would frequently call and ask how Ayesha was doing. I was continuously embarrassed.

As I slowly started to share the truth, it was comforting to hear how understanding everyone was. I was also surprised by how quickly people would open up to me.

"You can at least be thankful that it happened before the wedding and not after. I got divorced and it cleaned me up in lawyer fees," said one friend.

"My brother was engaged three different times and each one of them had the same result." said another.

It was amazing how often others will open up to you when they can relate. When my engagement came to a bitter end, I felt like I was the only one in my circle that went through this. I felt like a failure. After speaking with many others who experienced the same, I learned that these types of situations were more common than you'd think. People simply avoided discussing it in public.

I got back into my rhythm of personal growth: losing weight at the gym, reading books, listening to audio books on long drives, and learning from mentors like Darrell. This worked for me before, and I was certain that it would help once again.

Surprisingly, within a few weeks, I already started to get over Ayesha. I realized that I wasn't the same coffee-serving Mahfuz that thought his life was over after breaking off my first long-term relationship. This was a more mature and seasoned Mahfuz. I had my own independent goals and this slap in the face wasn't going to slow me down.

I learned (the hard way) that you can still hit mega roadblocks when things are going well. It's easy to have a positive attitude when things are going right, but a champion has a positive attitude when things are going very wrong.

I decided to live like a champion.

CHAPTER 21

THREE-PEAT

"If you aren't growing, you are dying"

I once heard a guest speaker share this message. I couldn't agree more.

Over the next few weeks, I would share this message through a series of speaking events. Wanting to practice what I preached, I continued picking up new books and learning from mentors.

To avoid overwhelming myself, I would spend time with my dad and repair the relationship with my family. To me, those moments with my dad were my most precious moments.

Growing didn't stop internally. Darrell and I continued growing the business.

Candybox now consisted of ten members and couldn't be more motivated to finish the year strong.

Working with an extremely talented team, we continued producing websites and marketing campaigns that we could be proud of. Businesses would choose our agency over much larger ones because of our culture and the quality of our work.

"We may not be the biggest, but we will be the best." Darrell always succeeded in putting his vision into perspective.

We were reinventing the digital marketing industry.

Over the last few years, I had received multiple job offers, from other marketing firms, but would quickly turn them down because of how much I loved what I did. However, I have to admit, it was very flattering hearing companies say things like: "you are the best account man I have ever met."

It was the time of year where associations would nominate marketing agencies for their outstanding work. This was our best year yet and I was confident that we had a shot.

Over the next few weeks, our team was thrilled to learn that Candybox has been nominated for three prestigious awards by different associations: Business Excellence Award, Young Entrepreneur of the Year Award, and the grand 2016 Entrepreneur of the Year Award.

This was amazing news but we knew that we would be competing with several other talented firms.

All three award shows would take place over the course of the same month and we were excited about the idea of going 3-for-3.

Darrell invited the team to join the festivities and, within a week, we found ourselves sitting together at an awards event, excited about the possibility of bringing home the Business Excellence Award.

After enjoying dinner and listening to an inspiring keynote speaker, the host stood in front of the podium to announce the winners.

"Candybox Marketing." He barely got to finish announcing the whole name before we jumped out of our seats in joy.

Our team marched up to the front of the room and was presented the award by the Governor General of Canada. I knew it was a moment I would never forget.

The month continued blessing us as we attended the other two events and celebrated with the same outcome.

Three awards in one month. It was a clean sweep!

The entrepreneur awards were provided to Darrell for his incredible work at Candybox Marketing. As someone who witnessed him build the company from ground up, I couldn't be prouder.

"Although this award is focused on being the Entrepreneur of the Year," Darrell said while delivering his speech. "I owe all of the success to the team that has been launching sweet websites in a high-pressure environment."

After celebrating with the team, we all took the time to write personal notes to clients and friends. This wouldn't have been possible without their support.

"Thank you for letting us do what we love!"

At this point in my life, I understood the definition of success. The definition of *my* success.

I thought about how society's definition of success was to get married in your early 20s, make babies, get a high paying job, and die old. This was the facade that created scary expectations for today's millennials.

Everyone's definition of success is unique and should be determined by their independent passion. Everyone can achieve success at their own pace. Life isn't a race.

My mistake was putting my happiness in the hands of a girl. Although I still look forward to getting married and having kids one day, I understood that lacking these would not classify me as a failure. I refused to let it define my success and happiness.

My passion was my family, my friends, building a business I loved, evolving to my full potential, and help others every step of the way.

I thought about the message I shared during my first speaking event: "if you want something bad enough, there are no challenges or obstacles that will stop you from getting it. This is your burning desire".

Take it from someone who had to learn this the hard way: no matter what stage you are in your life, determining your burning desire will allow you to thrive in all areas and overcome the most difficult challenges.

Once you discover your ultimate passion, you are equipped with the most powerful motivator to start reinventing yourself. This can be achieved through the following steps:

Step 1: Determine WHY you want to change. This is where your burning desire will fill in the blanks.

Step 2: Search for ways to achieve this transformation. There are several others out there who have already achieved this and can help you walk down the right path. Read books that share good ideas (like this one :-) and spend time with people who bring you closer to your goals. This leads me to step 3...

Step 3: Find the best mentors. I was lucky enough to find this through Darrell, Mike, and other incredible friends. This can fast-forward your personal growth and bring you back on track whenever you hit road blocks.

Step 4: Take action. Ideas and strategies on paper look great, but the execution is equally as important. Whether you spend time at the gym, start your own initiative, or simply take baby steps toward your goals, this is where the reinvention magic happens.

Step 5: Accept that shame, failure, and disappointments are temporary roadblocks that anyone can overcome. Your journey doesn't end when you are faced with challenges. Use Step 1 as fuel to keep you moving forward.

Step 6: Celebrate your smallest victories. You may find yourself being surprised by how quickly everything turns around once you start taking action. Take some time to celebrate the sweet successes during your journey.

No matter what my reinvention goals were, once I used these six steps, I became unstoppable.

Oh, and that vicious chatterbox that would constantly try to talk me out of things? I knew that it wasn't going away any time soon. I now understood that the chatterbox was just my overprotective conscious whose whole purpose was to protect me. This didn't mean that it always knew the best decisions. The greatest thrills came from silencing the chatterbox and proving it wrong.

It was my 31st birthday and Mike invited me to kick off the celebration with him and Jeannine.

> I don't want to overhype the gift, but I really think you are going to love it.
>
> Now I'm expecting the keys to your new Mustang!

I saw a couple wrapped gifts and was anxious to rip them open quicker than he could blink.

"Save the best one for last," Mike suggested while pointing at the larger gift.

Opening the first gift, I came across a hard cover book, breaking down the history of all comic book heroes and villains. Mike and I frequently would geek out over superheroes, so I looked forward to adding this to my collection.

I eyeballed the larger gift and prepared myself. After carelessly ripping apart the wrapping paper, I sat there speechless.

Staring back at me was a large portrait of one of the photographs we took during our car photo shoot. The photo displayed both of us standing beside our cars while engaged in conversation.

I always thought of Mike as the guy who has stuck with me through the most difficult hurdles in my life. It's still crazy to look back and think about the times when serving coffee in record time was our biggest challenge. We had both reached our own definition of success and couldn't be prouder of each other. This was the thought that was communicated to me every time I looked at this portrait sized photograph.

I looked at the incredible photo once again and summarized its meaning in three words:

We made it.

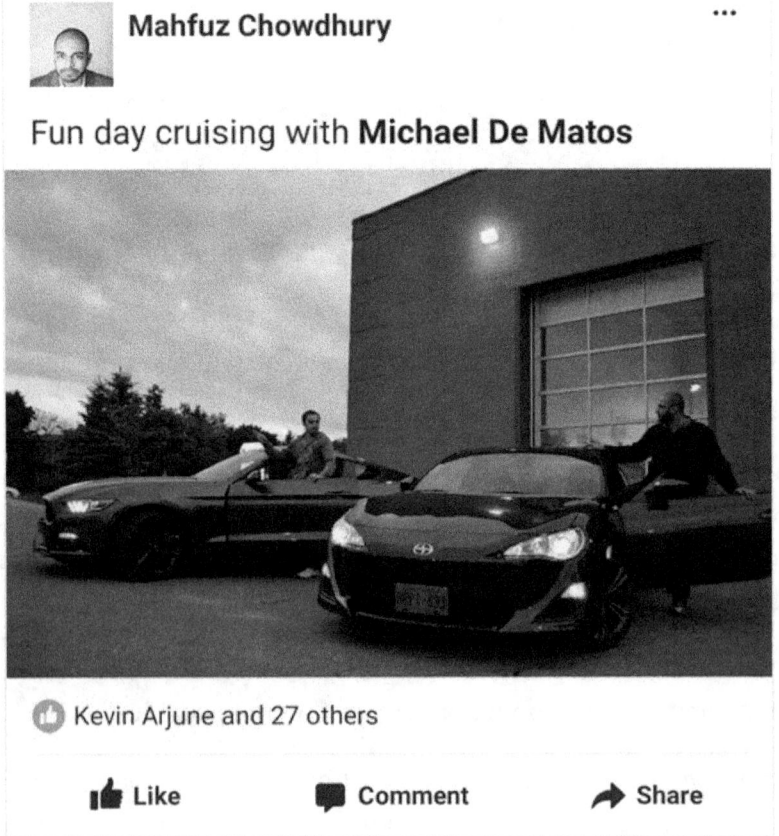

ENDING REMARKS

Progress was the name of the game.

Life moved forward for all of us. I would frequently connect with others to learn how everything was progressing.

My parents were living together in the same house I grew up in since this book started. My dad is healthier than he has been in a long time and my mom would remind me how proud she is of the man I have become.

Mike and Jeannine moved to a beautiful home in Stoney Creek and were still very much in love. We would make plans to meet each week to stay in touch and celebrate even our smallest wins in life. We recently celebrated Mike's birthday by taking a limo down to Niagara Falls. Knowing his love for Portugal and soccer, it was only fitting that I would give him a signed Ronaldo jersey as a gift.

Brendan pursued his passion for sales and got himself a great position at a local software company. He would always be one of the coolest guys I have ever met.

Mark graduated from college and landed a role as a teacher for high school students. He recently showed me a card that his students wrote to express how much they loved learning from him. With his fun personality, I had no doubt that the students would look forward to every class.

Argyle followed his love for computers and is working in the IT department for our city's police. He also recently got engaged to Rainie, who was also a member of the Sheridan STARs.

Marc never gave up on his passion for personal development.

He recently hitchhiked across Canada and wrote a book called 'Breaking Through'. Despite our differences, I was extremely proud of his success.

I could go on and on about how well the Glorious Gentlemen were doing. The entire group continued their personal growth and worked towards their definition of success. Some of them included: Kamil, who is currently living in Poland, completing his studies in medicine (and now has enough hair to make me jealous),

Romulo is preparing to take his policing exam this year, Jorge is currently employed as a videographer for a real estate company, and Brown went back to school to get the career of his dreams.

Darrell continued growing the Candybox Marketing team after our massive award-winning year. We are now a team of over 15 members and moved to a larger studio to accommodate everyone. Our team continues to reinvent the digital world, one website at a time.

As for me, I am currently writing this book from my new beautiful condo in Oakville. My enormous debt was no longer hanging over me as I paid it off during my early years at Candybox. You would still find me frequently speaking at events, or silently creating marketing strategies at my local Starbucks.

I hit my 6th year anniversary with Candybox and had to thank the one person who mentored me every step of the way.

> 6 years and I still feel like we are just hitting our stride!

> Excited for all the great things on the way! Endless thanks for the opportunity!!

> The pleasure is all mine. You're the best bet I've ever made!

I recently sat down with Brown to discuss my plans for this year.

> I think I'm finally ready to write that book.

> Yah, you have been talking about it since I met you.

> Well Brown, it's time to finally bring this idea to life.

The timing felt right. I wasn't a writer, but I had a story to share. I spent a lot of time removing the fluff to avoid losing focus of the timeline.

"Simple but significant," I often reminded myself.

What's next for me? Follow @mahfuzc on Instagram for the next chapter!

Until then, reinvent yourself.

www.ingramcontent.com/pod-product-compliance
Lightning Source LLC
LaVergne TN
LVHW051839080426
835512LV00018B/2958